I've had the privilege of talking with Daniel
him to have, not only vast personal experi
experience prophecy for themselves. That's
this book!

Having travelled the world ministering pr
rare to find resources on the prophetic tha
that are replicable on a local church level. This book IS that kind of resource.
Please do yourself a favour and let this book move you forward in the
prophetic. Do your church a favour, and implement this into your small
groups to help your people hear God's voice and share it with others!

Pastor Duane White
Apostolic Leader of the 02 Network of Churches and Ministries
Founding President of Beyond These Shores Ministries

I highly recommend Daniel's excellent book. It is one of the most practical
and inspiring books I have read on how to grow in the prophetic. He manages
to both inspire us with some jaw-dropping stories whilst also giving us very
helpful next steps along the way. As someone who works closely with him in
pastoral ministry, I can affirm Daniel lives what he writes. I believe that no
matter where you are at on the journey of finding and releasing your 'voice',
his book will help you take a next step.

Simon Deeks
Executive Pastor for Pastoral and Equip Ministry
KingsGate Church

For many, the concept of God speaking to them might appear strange or at
best, a very rare event. Daniel rightly presents the reader with an almighty,
transcendent God who is also very down-to-earth! That God could be saying
something to ordinary people like you and me is the gauntlet Daniel throws
down.

With self-deprecating humour, Daniel writes an immensely practical study of
how we can grow in our faithful attempts to discern with others what God
might be saying to us. Hearing that voice could change not only our own
lives, but also the lives of others as we learn to how to safely share what we
hear.

Dr Dave Emmett
Tutor in Theology
Emmanuel Theological College

VOICE

Hearing God's and Using Yours

Daniel Cole

O&U
Onwards & Upwards

Onwards and Upwards Publishers

4 The Old Smithy, London Road, Rockbeare,
EX5 2EA, United Kingdom.
www.onwardsandupwards.org

First edition, self-published in the United Kingdom by Daniel Cole (2022).

Second edition published in the United Kingdom by Onwards and Upwards Publishers (2023).

ISBN: 978-1-78815-959-3
Typeface: Sabon LT

About the Author

Daniel is a writer and speaker who loves to communicate godly principles in practical ways. He also serves as a pastor at KingsGate Community Church. With many years of pastoral and church leadership experience, Daniel is passionate about helping people reach their full potential in Christ.

Originally from Manchester, UK, he followed a call to relocate to Peterborough, UK, leaving behind a distinguished twenty-year career in property and asset management.

He is married to Rosy and they have four cheeky children.

Email:	voice@danielcole.uk
Facebook:	@daniel.cole.hello
Instagram:	@daniel.cole.hello
Blog:	lifewellbuilt.substack.com

Scan the QR code below to connect with Daniel on Facebook:

Dedication

I dedicate this book to Rosy, my true love and travelling partner.

Having you at my side as we've navigated challenging, difficult valleys as well as wonderful, breathtaking mountaintops has made it all worth it.

Here's to more crazy life adventures.

Contents

Foreword

Growing up in a Christian family often led me to be captivated and curious about God's voice. It was a noticeable family value for us to be open, expectant even, to hear God speak into our decisions and give us direction. It was not just in the big things either. I am not saying we would seek God's voice for whether we had rice or pasta for tea or what socks to wear, but there was an awareness. For example, when I was eleven, we were about to leave the house when I couldn't find my favourite yellow and green bobble hat that I wore all the time. I refused to leave without it. Mum, my five siblings and I searched the house from top to bottom, but still no joy. Finally, in the mayhem of the frantic hat hunt, Mum queried whether I had asked God where it was. In desperation to be reunited with my hat, I took a quiet minute and asked God. Instantly, I had a picture of my beloved hat. I ran up to my bedroom, put my hand down the side of the bed, and there it was, stuffed down and crumpled up.

Unqualified yet called

So, there was an awareness of God's voice throughout my childhood. Still, it was after an encounter with the Holy Spirit at nineteen that I began to receive a stirring and a sense of calling to use my voice – which deeply excited and utterly terrified me! Using my voice has been an epic battle, primarily

1

birthed from a tension of feeling unqualified yet called. On the one hand, there was an inner desire and passion to hear God's voice and share it with others, but on the other, I was being held back by feelings of inadequacy, unworthiness and being underqualified for the task. I've come to realise that I'm not alone in this. There are others who feel unqualified yet called. You might be one of them; Moses was another. He had all the ingredients to affirm his calling.

To begin with, he had his personal conviction to see change and freedom in his nation. He was also given a supernatural sign in a burning bush. God threw in a couple of extras by displaying His power with two miracles just for Moses to see. If that wasn't enough to bolster Moses' boldness, God, well, you know, actually called him – specifically and directly called him. In the clearest of terms, He said, "Now go, I am sending you..."[1] Moses' response is not what you would expect – laughable even, but honestly, I get it. The Bible recalls his responses to include "Who am I?", "Please send someone else", "I have never been eloquent" and "I am slow of speech and tongue".[2] Do you see the 'unqualified yet called' tension? I had used these same excuses countless times when I heard God's voice for someone and bottled out from using my voice. When I first read this passage many years ago, I thought to myself, *you've literally taken these words out of my mouth.*

But, do you know Moses used his voice? He overcame the barriers of inadequacy and stepped into his calling. He spoke God-breathed words to the highest rulers on earth in the intimacy of a majestic palace. He spoke to vast multitudes in

---

[1]   Exodus 3:10
[2]   Exodus 4:10

the expanse of the wilderness. With much less drama and glamour than Moses, it has been this similar tension that I have grappled with in overcoming the barriers to using my voice for communicating God's voice.

Over time, I have come to see beauty in this tension. To carry that sense of calling in the light of our human weakness means a need to be reliant on God's grace and power. We rely not on our works or achievements but on His mercy and love for us. Apostle Paul said to the Corinthian church that he did not use his voice with eloquence, or persuasive or wise words, as he proclaimed about God,[3] but in his weaknesses, he relied heavily on the power of the Spirit. Peter and John were being held to account with questions from the rulers and elders of Jerusalem for using their voices to proclaim salvation and healing. The Bible says they were astonished by their courage to speak as well as they did, particularly as they were unschooled, ordinary men.[4] It says the reason was clear; they had been with Jesus. Being with Jesus, growing in our intimacy with Him and from that place using our voices for His glory – that's what it's all about, living in this 'unqualified yet called' tension.

A gift

It's not just a calling; it's a gift. A gift called prophecy. It is a gift available to all. You can hear God's voice and use yours to bring hope, love and encouragement into the world around you. This book will help you engage with this wonderful gift. It's written to unpack what I have learnt from living in this tension: some of the stories, mistakes, shortcomings, successes,

---

[3]   1 Corinthians 2:4
[4]   Acts 4:13

character growth opportunities; and of course, some eternal biblical truths were thrown in for good measure! The purpose of it all is to pass on some principles and passion that would stir the gift of prophecy within you for His glory and purposes.

What is the story with your voice? Extrovert or introvert? Eloquent or slow of speech? Speaking of mysteries and riddles or in normal sentences? Whatever your tendency or personality style is, whether you're comfortable on the platform or in the coffee shop, this book will show that you have the God-given ability to use your voice to express and communicate God's love and purposes here on earth. It will prove to you that the gift of prophecy is available to you today.

Disclaimer

I write this foreword as more of a disclaimer. It's to let you know that this book has not been written from a prophetic mountaintop, and I'm not a particularly seasoned writer or theologian. Honestly, I am an introvert who frequently trips over my words and certainly I have many moments of ineloquence. I often stutter, mutter, get stage fright and have mind blanks and nerves like you wouldn't believe. I have battled with low self-confidence and low self-esteem. I have faced spiritual oppression where the enemy has tried to keep me quiet. For a season, I had a very tangible fear of my own voice. (I know I share this at risk of deflating any sense of faith and expectation you had for the book!) So, hang in there, and if you make it past the foreword, you will hopefully see in the following pages that if God can use my voice, He will certainly and undeniably use yours!

The book is grounded in biblical principles, delving into many key scriptures and key themes related to prophecy. It has revelatory insights and also actionable processes.

It is split into two sections: the first part focuses on 'God's Voice', and the second focuses on 'Your Voice'.

It has been very much written with practical application in mind, which includes:

- Small group resources at the end of chapters 2-7
- Personal 'Voice Check' assessment
- Reflective questions for personal study
- Summary of key verses
- Activation and ministry tools

I pray this will be a practical tool to help unlock your prophetic potential and a resource for growth in prophetic gifting.

As we get started, let me again underline that God has plenty to say, and He has created us with the ability to speak. He intends to put the two together. Will we hear His voice, and will we use ours?

Introduction

> A voice of one calling in the wilderness: prepare the way for the Lord...[5]

Go back in time with me and imagine you're an ancient eastern King or Queen, living in your lavish palace with all the rich, royal trappings at your disposal. Then one day, you're called to visit another city, meaning you must leave behind your comfortable surroundings and travel across an uninhabited wilderness desert. It is not the most enjoyable experience for anyone, believe me. I went on a brief excursion riding a camel across the Sahara Desert on my honeymoon. Let's just say I had saddle pain for several days afterwards and haven't been on a camel since! Well, historians tell us that to make this unpractised and, at times, unpassable journey across the trackless desert as tolerable as possible, the expedition would send teams on ahead to prepare the way for a more pleasant experience. This team of harbingers removed hindrances and worked to strengthen pathways or soften impediments.

Voice

One of their most critical jobs, though, was to use their voices. This was to shout announcements ahead, advising any approaching groups about who was soon to pass through. They

---

[5] Isaiah 40:3

also shouted back to the party about upcoming issues that might impact them and provided updates and possible course corrections. An ancient sat nav, if you will.

A voice calling

So, imagine you're sitting on your camel, with gusts of wind blowing sand in all your nooks and crannies, monitoring your rapidly decreasing supplies and enduring the bumps and jolts of the challenging terrain. But then your ears begin to pick up the sound of voices piercing through the air. Perhaps faint voices at first as they echo from a distance, but which become clearer and sharper as you keep pushing forwards. Gradually, you can make out what the messengers are communicating: the solutions to passageway problems, limitations lifted as pathways have been levelled, breakthroughs into ways where blockages have been removed and new directions to progress forward.

In effect, the voices of these heralds calling in the desert significantly helped keep the journey moving forward and provided safe arrivals.

It is this factual imagery that the prophet Isaiah is drawing from when he hears God's voice and uses his to convey this message to the Israelites:

A voice of one calling in the wilderness: prepare the way for the LORD; make straight in the desert a highway for our God. Every valley shall be raised up, every mountain and hill made low; the rough ground shall become level, the rugged places a plain. And the glory of the LORD will be revealed, and all people will see it together. For the mouth of the LORD has spoken.[6]

Being the herald in the desert, Isaiah himself encouraged God's people that their Babylonian captivity would not last, but a time of freedom was coming. It is, of course, also a messianic promise of the coming Jesus, who would bring freedom to all mankind. John the Baptist picks up this sentiment too. He set up a home in the wilderness, and when his identity was questioned, he answered by repeating Isaiah word for word.[7]

Your voice is calling

Now, before you conclude that I think we need to be more like John the Baptist, wearing camel hair clothing with a diet of wild honey and locusts, my point is that you have a voice, whatever your context is, wilderness or otherwise.

It has been designed to help you and others navigate the ups and downs of this journey we call life. It can help remove hindrances, unblock obstacles, get you on track and move you forward in the right direction. From the outset, my encouragement is to settle in your heart that you, like Isaiah and John the Baptist, are called to hear God's voice and use yours. You can be that herald, that voice, calling out the things of God in your context. In fact, Isaiah goes on to say, "You who bring good news to Jerusalem, lift up your voice with a shout, lift it up, do not be afraid..."[8]

---

[6] Isaiah 40:4-5
[7] John 1:23
[8] Isaiah 40:9

Be present and prepared

It's a damp, rainy morning on 26th June 2019, which is not uncommon in Manchester. I've risen early to spend some time in prayer before the hustle and bustle of our four children waking up, wandering downstairs and wanting breakfast – all part of the usual school morning routine. I very much appreciate the early peace in the house before chaos ensues! Anyway, here I am in prayer on this rainy morning, and I simply hear the following words whispered in my spirit: "Kings, Peterborough, Dave and Karen".

Having no idea what they meant or even where Peterborough was, I took my prayer time to Google! Entering "Kings, Peterborough, Dave and Karen" into the search engine brought to the top of the list a church called KingsGate Community Church. Where was it? In Peterborough.

I go on the website and see the senior leaders are... Dave and Karen. Wow, that's got my attention! This holy moment of me, God and Google is soon interrupted by the pattering of the children's feet coming down the stairs, and I wonder how on earth I will organise the breakfasts and make the packed lunches, all while processing what I've just heard!

This led to a family adventure of working with the word, receiving wise counsel from trusted people and connecting with Dave, Karen and others at KingsGate. Cutting a long story short, in January 2020, I left my twenty-year property career, relocated to Peterborough and joined the staff team.

A friend recently asked me how God spoke to me so clearly. My gut response to him was that I had to learn to be present and prepared. So, to fully embrace the invitation of hearing

God and using our voice for His glory, these are two cornerstones to build on in readiness for what's in the following pages.

Be present

This particular word fell in an interesting season for Rosy and me. We had sensed in the summer of 2018 that 2019 would be a year of change for us, with no particular plans or conclusions, just an inner expectation. Before we could even form plans, the latter months of 2018 and the beginning of 2019 turned out to be gruelling and challenging times. This was partly due to internal circumstances within our church community, which were outside our control or understanding. I was also made redundant at work too – great timing! I found a job relatively quickly, which solved one problem, but on the church front, we ended up leaving. We found ourselves grieving for our church family and constantly over-processing and trying to make sense of it all. At the same time, our heads were spinning with a stack of unanswered questions about our future. Trapped between our past and future, we were unravelling quickly until, one day, we drew a line in the sand and decided to focus on the present. Easier said than done. We had to make a daily decision to quieten the voices of the past and the future and live in the present. We were to become available for what the day ahead had for us, disciplining our thought life, our prayer life and our late-night conversations to remain in the present. It was only then, in the quietness and contentedness of the present, that God spoke about our future.

Have you unanswered questions regarding not hearing or mishearing God's voice? Or looking forward, do you have a desire to hear God more clearly? Or perhaps an unfulfilled passion to use your voice to impact your world? Whatever voices of your past or future may be going around your head and heart, decide to be present. Take some time to prayerfully settle in your heart or write in your journal a commitment to focus on today. Read this book from a place of peace in the present and allow God to minister to you afresh.

Be prepared

So, Rosy and I let go of the past and any future concerns and remained in the present. Remember, God hadn't spoken about our future at this point. I could have easily filled my time with Netflix or social media. Just some of my time was on this; after all, I am human. However, what I did was choose to continue showing up for my time with God; to keep my heart and spirit softened, prepared and available to hear Him. I find it interesting that, in this instance, God gave this life-altering word during my regular morning prayer time. There is no substitute for keeping a prepared heart than the healthy habits of time with God through the Bible and prayer.

How can you prepare for God to have His way in you? This is the premise of Isaiah's message: "Prepare the way of the Lord." Let this be a personal encouragement to you. Is there some preparation work to be done on the highways of your thought life that might need straightening out? Maybe for you, it's preparation work on any rough ground in your heart that might then become the fertile soil for God to minister.

Before we get into chapter one, a simple, reflective 'voice check' might help you become present and prepared as we go on this exciting journey of hearing His voice and using ours. It is a practical assessment you can refer back to and share with others.

Voice Check Assessment

Give yourself a score between 1 (low) and 10 (high). Once you have a total, read through the score results. Complete it instinctively, giving your gut responses rather than overthinking it. The goal is to help you find areas of strength and growth.

GOD'S VOICE

Hearing God comes quite easily to me.

(1) (2) (3) (4) (5) (6) (7) (**8**) (9) (10)

I strongly understand why God chooses to speak to me.

(1) (2) (3) (4) (5) (6) (7) (**8**) (9) (10)

I can identify God speaking to me in various ways.

(1) (2) (3) (4) (5) (6) (7) (**8**) (9) (10)

I listen to God by intentionally putting specific time aside.

(1) (2) (3) (4) (**5**) (6) (7) (8) (9) (10)

I listen to God as I go about my day in conversation with Him.

(1) (2) (3) (4) (5) (6) (7) (**8**) (9) (10)

Add the scores together to give you a total: __37__

Scores of 5-10

There are some areas needing attention to unlock more of hearing His voice.

Scores of 11-25

There is some understanding and experience in hearing God; however, more can be developed.

Scores of 26-37

You have a good understanding and some good practices in hearing God. Consider some tweaks to go to a new level.

Scores of 38-45

You are extremely attentive, intentional and creative in hearing God often. Find ways to help others.

Scores of 46-50

You imitate Jesus – always hearing the Father's voice!

YOUR VOICE

I am quite confident in using my voice.

(1) (2) (3) (4) (5) (6) (7) (8) (9) (10)

What I say and my faith are closely connected.

(1) (2) (3) (4) (5) (6) (7) (8) (9) (10)

I strongly understand the 'gift of prophecy'.

(1) (2) (3) (4) (5) (6) (7) (8) (9) (10)

I have trusted people around me to help me practise the prophetic safely.

(1) (2) (3) (4) (5) (6) (7) (8) (9) (10)

I understand the power of using my voice outside of the church context.

(1) (2) (3) (4) (5) (6) (7) (8) (9) (10)

Add the scores together to give you a total: ___39___

Scores of 5-10

There are some areas needing attention to unlock more of using your voice.

Scores of 11-25

Though you've had some experience being prophetic, there is more to develop.

Scores of 26-37

You often use the gift of prophecy and have confidence in using your voice. Consider some tweaks to go to a new level.

Scores of 38-45

You are very confident about using your voice. Connect with others and find trusted people.

Scores of 46-50

You imitate Jesus – always speaking the Father's words!

1
Send Me

And I said, "Here I am. Send me!"[9]

Next time you buy a stamp and send a letter, think about Rowland Hill.[10] Rowland was an English teacher in the 1830s who got fed up with the inadequate and expensive postal service of the day.

The service of sending and delivering messages dates back to 1516 when Henry VIII established a 'Master of Posts'. But in the 1800s, the postal service fell into disrepute with poor management and wasteful systems.

The story goes that Rowland's frustration really hit home one day when he saw a poor young woman unable to claim a letter from her fiancé. This frustration grew, leading him to take a serious interest in the postal service. As he dug deeper by researching books and documents, he uncovered many problems across the board, including significant fraud at every level, high levels of unpaid delivery debts and, conclusively, a broken system.

---

[9]   Isaiah 6:8
[10] wikipedia.org/wiki/Rowland_Hill

Eventually, in 1837, Rowland submitted a proposal to the government called 'Post Office Reform: its importance and practicability',[11] which after two years of it being denounced and unsupported by politicians, they then agreed to try the new system in 1839. Rowland got himself a new job and calling.

In the simplest terms, the proposal was this: the sender pays the postal charge, not the receiver.

By essentially putting the onus on the sender, Rowland revolutionised how we send mail. This change started in England, which included the first adhesive postage stamp,[12] and then was caught by many other countries who established the same systems within their national services. Rowland changed the face of the global postal system, which we still enjoy today. In fact, the UK's postal service (Royal Mail) stated in its March 2021 annual report that 9.5 billion letters had been sent.[13] In other words, that's roughly 26 million letters per day on average, which is a lot of messages being sent; thanks to Rowland!

The onus is on the sender

Every prophetic message you have the privilege to deliver is heaven-sent. It has God's stamp of approval attached to it and has been given to you to distribute and deliver.

---

[11] Eleanor C. Smyth, Sir Rowland Hill; *The Story of a Great Reform;* HardPress (2017)
[12] postalmuseum.org/collections/rowland-hill-postal-reforms
[13] statista.com/statistics/1006816/royal-mail-volume-of-parcels-and-letters-delivered-uk

You are the delivery person – a sender of messages. *Here I am. Send me!*

Isaiah was a sender of messages slightly before Rowland Hill brought reforms. He conveyed some outstanding, eternal prophetic words. We saw Isaiah, in the Introduction, being the voice in the desert and calling out to the people of God.[14] He proclaimed that salvation was coming in their present situation, but which we know was also a foreshadow regarding their and our eternal destiny. In referring to this prophecy in Mark 1:2, Jesus actually uses the term, "I will send my 'messenger' ahead of you…" Such was the influence of Isaiah's messages that Jesus quotes from him five times in the Book of Matthew.[15] Paul also quotes Isaiah in his New Testament writings.[16] I suppose one is not of minor importance when referenced by two world changers like Jesus and Paul!

However, prophesying at this measure wasn't always the case. There was a turning point for Isaiah, much like the global reformational turning point of the postal services in 1839. Rowland stood up to be counted in for the calling of transformation. For Isaiah, he had a heavenly experience, leading him to stand up and say, "Here I am. Send me."

A lot happened in Isaiah's moment of reformation and calling, which is found in Isaiah 6. This Isaiah 6 experience can also help us as we embrace the gift of prophecy. Before we get into that, I just want to note that there is a beautiful communication among all the sounds, colours, movements and visuals.

---

[14] Isaiah 40:3
[15] Matthew 3:3, 4:14, 8:17, 12:17, 13:14, 15:17
[16] Romans 9:27, 9:29, 10:16, 10:20, 15:12

Isaiah heard God's voice and then used his.

It's a question from God and a response from Isaiah. It's an intimate interaction within all the heavenly cacophony – a private back and forth. Yet, there is something of a relationship forming and closeness in the communication. Isaiah is clearly in awe and wonder as God asks, "Whom shall I send? And who will go for us?"[17] But he is humbled and submissive, even as he answers back, "Here I am. Send me."

It is the same for you. Being prophetic is hearing God's voice and, in response, using yours. Use your voice to speak back your response to God: "Here I am. Send me."

Before we look at what 'send me' looks like, though, I'm going to share some thoughts on what it looks like to be prophetic like Isaiah.

In awe

...I saw the Lord...[18]

Being prophetic is being a worshipper. It is to encounter Him, to behold His majesty and wonder in worship. It is in this context of worship that Isaiah had his 'send me' moment.

King Uzziah's death was a blow, because under his rule, the people prospered brilliantly.[19] They were victorious in war and overall enjoyed a time of peace and well-being. However, there was a period of uncertainty and unrest as the kingship was

---

[17] Isaiah 6:8-9
[18] Isaiah 6:1
[19] Alexander MacLaren; *MacLaren On The Bible: Alexander MacLaren's Exposition Of Holy Scripture*

being transferred to his son and successor, Jotham. With all this going on in the backdrop, Isaiah had a vision of seeing the Lord. His focus was taken off the natural and earthly kings to behold and worship the King of all kings who is high and exalted, seated on the throne.

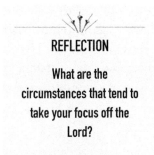

REFLECTION

What are the circumstances that tend to take your focus off the Lord?

While there are many kinds of transitions and movements in the circumstances of life, being prophetic is looking above it all and seeing the Lord. At the heart of prophecy is encountering the heart of God. It is stepping into a place of awe and wonder as we see Him in all His glory, as Isaiah did.

It is often very easy to get into a prayer mode, asking God for His word on a certain matter – a surface-level, quick fix, grabbing for God's word for a solution – nipping in and out of His presence. By His grace, He will sometimes still speak to us in this way. He has to me when my relationship with Him has been shallow. Nevertheless, we must know that the primary goal is not to hear His voice but to catch His heart and see His face. Hearing His voice is simply one of the wonderful outcomes. If we look for His face, it won't be difficult to hear His voice!

Isaiah isn't the only one who has a worshipful, prophetic encounter. The Lord called Samuel to be His messenger to the people while he was sleeping in the temple. The temple is the place on earth where God's presence would descend, a place very familiar with the hymns and hallelujahs of heaven. Samuel responded with, "Speak, for your servant is listening."[20] The Lord encountered Moses through a burning bush, a fire synonymous with His presence. God mandated him to be His messenger of freedom to the captives, and Moses, from this place of encounter, responded with, "Here I am."[21]

As well as all three responding with "Here I am", Samuel, Moses and Isaiah all had this in common: they were all prophetic messengers sent from God's presence.

You too can step into an encounter with God and pray this simple prayer, "Here I am."

Being prophetic means not missing this step of the encounter. Because prophecy flows from a place of worship and encounter, we must first step into His presence to step out into the prophetic.

Isaiah saw and heard the eternal sound of countless angels singing *holy, holy, holy*.[22] Their unified voices surrounded the throne in worshipful adoration and awe of the King. In the Book of Revelation, John gets a similar heavenly glimpse approximately one thousand years later.[23] Worship extends outside of the parameters of time and echoes through eternity. Being prophetic is engaging with this worship. It is rising above earthly limitations and, like Isaiah, joining with the angelic beings to simply see the Lord. It is to gaze upon His face and stand in awe, making His presence our priority.

---

[20] 1 Samuel 3:1-10
[21] Exodus 3:4
[22] Isaiah 6:3
[23] Revelation 4:8

Raising awareness

What does stepping into His presence mean practically? I think it is about living in a continual awareness of Him. Every believer will have some awareness of God, but not always at a conscious level. It is learning to develop that intimacy consistently.

These three Old Testament foreshadows that I've just mentioned reveal God's heart to come close to us as He calls us into our destiny as heaven-sent messengers. Through Jesus, we now have the privilege of hosting His presence. We have His Spirit living within us whereby we can walk every step by the Spirit.[24] You can't get much closer than that. We can have a lifestyle of worship and adoration to God in which we are continually aware of His presence with us and in us. We can experience Spirit-led worship and encounters as we open ourselves up regularly towards Him. His Spirit enables us to hear His voice and use ours. Prophecy is, after all, a gift of the Spirit.

Bill Johnson says, "We must adjust whatever is necessary to rediscover the practical nature of the presence of God."[25]

As we rediscover or develop our awareness of God's presence, I've already introduced two practical ways through which we can adjust, just as Bill Johnson encourages us to do. These are being present and being prepared. I don't want to labour these points too much, but they both very much apply to being a prophetic worshipper.

---

[24] Galatians 5:25
[25] Bill Johnson; *Hosting the Presence;* Destiny Image (2012)

One of my sons listed 'professional football player' as one of his top three career choices. This is a great ambition, though I have to give him a nudge every now and then. I have to remind him that instead of online gaming and such like, to be a professional footballer, you've got to show up and practise. If you want to master the sport, you've got to be present and prepared. I tell him that though I will do all I can to help his journey, "I am not going to work harder than you." You might think this is harsh parenting, but the reality is he is not going to develop his skill if it's just me out in the garden showing up and practising. I'll improve (which is no bad thing) but he won't!

Likewise, let me encourage you: get super practical! Look for adjustments that would allow you to be present in His presence. Prepare your heart and mind to fix your eyes on Him in worship and open your ears to hear Him.

When I am weak

> "Woe to me!" I cried. "I am ruined! For I am a man of unclean lips, and I live among a people of unclean lips, and my eyes have seen the King, the LORD Almighty."[26]

Being prophetic is being a worshipper. It is also relying on His strength. Isaiah becomes very aware of his human frailty and weaknesses in God's presence. It's interesting that he chooses only one weakness in this holy moment of confessing his possible shortcomings and character flaws (I would have a long list!) – his mouth. There is something about surrendering our voices to God, even confessing before Him and repenting for where our voices have fallen short. We can find His strength to

---

[26] Isaiah 6:5

speak from this place of acknowledging our weakness and surrender.

I've already shared in the Foreword that my voice has been a weakness to me; not necessarily due to foul or negative language, but due to insecurity and a lack in confidence. I knew I had the potential within me to be prophetic, yet I kept silent and hid behind the lies of inadequacy and fear – that 'unqualified yet called' tension.

Admitting our weakness takes vulnerability. It takes guts to come out of our fears and any masks we've been hiding behind and lay them bare before God. But "our willingness to own and engage with it will determine the depth of our courage and the clarity our of purpose"[27]. There is no safer place to let it all out than in God's presence.

I resolved to overcome the obstacles and break through the blockages regarding my voice. I worked harder to talk in uncomfortable settings and pushed myself to share in group settings. I strived to speak in front of crowds. Of course, my heart was in the right place, but I nevertheless struggled on in my own strength.

These practical elements helped to some degree in terms of forming habits and disciplines. However, the breakthrough came when I surrendered my voice and laid my weakness before God in prayer; as the Message Translation puts it, "Every word I've ever spoken is tainted—blasphemous even!"[28] A little extreme, but you get the picture!

---

[27] Brene Brown; *Daring Greatly;* Penguin (2012)
[28] Isaiah 6:5 (MSG)

Humble pie

Being prophetic is recognising our weaknesses and relying on His strength. Bowing our knees and surrendering our voice to Him is humbling, but it's the only way.

Isaiah captures this prophetic correlation between our knees and our voices in one of his latter prophecies:

> Before me every knee will bow; by me every tongue will swear. They will say of me, 'In the LORD alone are deliverance and strength.'[29]

I love how this wasn't just an abstract message but something he had profoundly and personally experienced. Paul quotes this passage to the church in Rome, describing how we should present ourselves before God.[30] And to the Philippi church, he explains that we must all take on the same humility of Christ. Jesus, who once humbled Himself to death, now sits in the highest place. And catch this; he says, "...at the name of Jesus every knee should bow ... and every tongue acknowledge that Jesus Christ is Lord..."[31] There it is again. We bow our knees and we use our voices. From a bowed knee and a surrendered voice to the lordship of Jesus, flows strength. There is a divine order at work: when I am weak, then I am strong.[32]

The power to prophetically use your voice is made perfect in weakness. Isaiah's story can be your story. Your voice can be powerful as it relies on His strength.

---

[29] Isaiah 45:23
[30] Romans 14:11
[31] Philippians 2:10-11
[32] 2 Corinthians 12:10

Being prophetic is being a worshipper and relying on His strength. It is also being free.

A used saucepan

A good friend of mine once illustrated that living in freedom was like a used saucepan, and there are three stages to cleaning it. There is soaking the pan to loosen any tough debris stuck to the insides. Then, there's scrubbing and wash-

REFLECTION

Take a pause to bow your knees and offer up your mouth to God. Surrender your voice to Him. Repent, if needed, where you have used your voice outside of His lordship.

ing to make it clean. Finally, once it's clean, it's to be wiped down, dried off and inspected, before being placed back in the cupboard. There is some truth in this three-stage approach. Isaiah's experience is actually not dissimilar to the used pan. He goes through the three stages, as it were, before knowing the freedom to receive his prophetic calling.[33]

1. PURIFIED

   …with a live coal … [the angel] touched my mouth…

(The soaking stage)

The saucepan is filled with hot water to break down the grease and grime build-up that is stubbornly stuck around the edges of the pan. The heat of the water eventually softens the residual debris so that it can be washed away, just like the heat from the coal in Isaiah's vision touching His lips as a symbol of purification. It is meant to burn away the dross. It is this heating

---

[33] Isaiah 6:6-7

element that's important. Again, Paul picks this up. This is not about heating a saucepan, but he talks about being tested by fire![34] This is burning away the unnecessary and the unwanted, with what remains being the things that would withstand the tests.

It reminds me of Shadrach, Meshach and Abednego thrown into the blazing furnace, firmly tied up for not worshipping the false god. It was a fire so hot that the guards who took them died from the heat. Yet, we're told they were seen unbound, unharmed and walking around with a fourth person by their side.[35] They survived the testing fire because of their purity of devotion and faith in God.

Like Shadrach, Meshach and Abednego, Isaiah goes through a purifying experience as the burning coal touches his mouth.

The dictionary defines 'purified' as "contaminants removed, free from objectionable elements"[36].

What's your purification process? How can you remain in a posture of "clean hands and a pure heart"[37]? I would suggest that holiness is a key. As the angelic chorus of *holy, holy, holy* rings out, I think Isaiah is taken aback by the holiness of God, perhaps with a burning desire to be holy like He is holy.[38] We become like what we worship. By concentrating on His holiness through our worship, we become more like Him, and not only

---

[34] 1 Corinthians 3:13
[35] Daniel 3
[36] dictionary.com/browse/purified
[37] Psalm 24:4
[38] 1 Peter 1:15

that, it shields our ear and eye gates from things that could allow unholiness to gain entrance.

I'm sure, like me, you have tried to clean the muck off the saucepan with some grit and elbow grease, which is much harder than simply letting it sit in some hot water for a while. In the same way, resting in the power and purity of God's presence by His grace will bring us significantly more freedom than our own efforts could ever do.

2. GUILT GOES

"...your guilt is taken away..."

(The cleaning stage)

The running of water as the grease and grime leave the saucepan and disappear down the drain means they cannot return back up. They're gone. I love the phrase used in the passage: "taken away".

Let me briefly return to my John the Baptist parallel from the Introduction. As I covered, when his identity and motivation were questioned, he repeated Isaiah's words verbatim: "I am the voice of one calling in the wilderness, 'Make straight the way for the Lord.'"[39] It's obvious that John is a huge Isaiah fan. I'm convinced he would have had an 'I heart Isaiah' T-shirt on, if he weren't wearing camel's hair.

The passage says that the next day John saw the Lord (like Isaiah did) and announced, "Look, the Lamb of God, who

---

[39] John 1:23

takes away the sin of the world!"[40] There is that phrase (like Isaiah): "takes away". Told you – a huge fan!

God takes away Isaiah's sin, and as John (like Isaiah) rightly points out, Jesus came to take away our sin. Sin is a blockage that separates us from God. Guilt is a feeling that keeps us distant from His voice and reluctant to use ours. Jesus can wash away that sin mess and help clean up the guilt too. It is simply a matter of repenting. It is saying sorry to God for that thing we may have done wrong; He will take it away by His grace and goodness. He will make us holy by washing us clean with water.[41]

Asking Him to take away those burdens of sin and guilt through repentance will make you wonderfully free to hear His voice more clearly and use your voice as well.

3. FORGIVENESS COMES

"...your sin atoned for."

(The wipe down and inspect stage)

The grease and grime are gone. The saucepan is clean, and now we grab a towel, give it a check over and make it sparkle. This stage is about making sure there are no remnants of the last meal left. This is about learning to truly let go of the past grease and grime. The New Living Translation uses the word 'forgiven' in this passage, which simply means cancelling the debt for an offence, flaw or mistake.

---

[40] John 1:29
[41] Ephesians 5:26

Of course, we see God cancelling Isaiah's debt here, and He is quick to forgive us too. Being prophetic is being free, and part of this is walking in that forgiveness. As we have freely received it, we freely give it to those who have offended us.

I'll briefly talk about forgiveness later in the book, but for now, I would just say that harbouring unforgiveness can limit the gift of prophecy.

Unforgiveness keeps you listening to the messages and experiences of your past that caused you pain and hurt rather than having a sharper focus on the heaven-sent messages you are called to deliver to your world. It is possible to listen to both, but it limits you. Trust me, I've tried. When I surrendered my voice to God and recognised my weakness, part of this was learning to forgive those in my past. I went to counselling to help navigate this pain and find healing. Cancelling the debt of those past voices set me up to be ready and available to hear His and use mine at a whole new level of freedom.

The saucepan has been purified, washed and wiped down. It's an available, empty vessel ready for use. Now we arrive at Isaiah's "send me" moment.

REFLECTION

Don't particularly go searching for past pain or hurt, but ask God to reveal anything that you might be holding on to. Let Him guide you. Ask others to stand with you in this too. Perhaps seek professional help if appropriate.

Quick responder

> Then I heard the voice of the Lord saying, "Whom shall
> I send? And who will go for us?" And I said, "Here I
> am. Send me!"

Rosy and I have a running joke in our house that we inherited
from Rosy's mum, who has a mischievous sense of humour.
Whenever one of us calls out to the other around the house,
and they don't want to respond, they'll retort something like,
"Sorry, can't hear you; the tap is running" or "the washing
machine is on" or "the hoover is on". Sometimes, this is true –
we can't hear them because of background noise – but mostly,
it's not. It's just a joke to avoid responding to what will likely
be an impending request from the other! It's becoming less
funny now, though, as the kids have picked it up, with retorts
like, "Sorry, can't hear you; my phone is vibrating" or "the cat
is meowing"!

When I read this passage in Isaiah, the impression I get is the
promptness of Isaiah's response. No excuses. No whirring
washing machines or running taps to hide behind. It was a
confident, positive "Send me!"

As God asks the question, I imagine Isaiah going from bowing
the knee posture to standing up to attention. Guilt has been
taken away, and forgiveness has come. He now stands with his
shoulders up and back straightened. He hears God's voice and,
with fresh hope and expectation, responds quickly with his.

This is the same posture we can take as we consider the
prophetic, not just in a single moment but on an ongoing basis.
When God gives you prophetic messages, don't wait or make

excuses. Instead, step out in faith and deliver the message. Be a quick responder. Remain in a heart posture of 'send me'.

Now, back to the postal service and the onus changing to the sender. In his desire to use his voice, I wonder if Isaiah got too self-absorbed ("Woe to me! … I am a man of unclean lips…") The focus is unbalanced toward the deliverer and not the sender. We can all relate to this, I'm sure. It's like a disproportionate focus towards my voice; that is, what could have been said clearer, with better timing or not said at all? Perhaps where have we missed it, lost, overused or misused it? Rowland Hill flipped the postal service on its head by giving the responsibility to the sender. God flips the script with us. He turns it around. The onus is on Him, the sender. It's His messages we are called to deliver. We can simply come before Him with open ears and an open heart that says, "Here I am. Send me." Switching the focus of our voice causes us to draw strength and power from the sender.

Can we always get it right? In my experience, not at all, and that's okay. The key is in the 'send me' response. This speaks of heart – a desire to come back to God's presence and bow the knee before Him in awe. It is giving Him our voice in surrender. It speaks of emptying what doesn't belong – then standing up with humility and going again. In your prophetic endeavours, put the onus on the sender.

Go and tell

After Isaiah says, "Send me," God then says, "Go and tell…"[42] Essentially, God is forming His job description, giving him His

---

[42] Isaiah 6:9

REFLECTION

Meditate on and then pray into John 20:21. Thank God for the love He has for you as His child. Pray that you might know a fresh sense of commission in the whole area of prophecy.

objectives. *You need to go and you need to tell. Go to the Israelites with my authority as my ambassador and use your voice to tell them the messages I am asking you to deliver.*

GO

When the postal service changes were being implemented in 1837-39, they needed to change the stamping process to reflect that the letter had been prepaid. The idea they conceived was to use a "glutinous wash"[43] to affix the stamp to the front of the letter. It would have an emblem of the Monarch's head as well. This 'Penny Black' stamp would prove that the sender had paid for and authorised its delivery.

The stamp is fixed on the letter. You have the King of Kings' stamp of approval on your lips. You have been given all authority in heaven and on earth to go.[44] Receive the prophetic commissioning to go with His authority.

One of my favourite verses in the Bible fits in well here, when Jesus says, "As the father sends me, so I send you."[45] Wow! It means we've been sent in the authority, power and intimacy of the Father... just like Jesus. Let that sink in a minute. You have

---

[43] postalmuseum.org/collections/Rowland-hill-postal-reforms
[44] John 20:21
[45] Matthew 28:18

been sent from heaven to carry the words of God that can bring life transformation.

TELL

It's one thing to go; it's another to tell. We are to use our voice and tell others what we sense God is saying. Isaiah is instructed to specifically tell. Other definitions for this Hebrew word are "call out, declare, plainly say, still say, utter"[46]. The first mention of this word is at the start of the Bible in creation. It's the thirty-eighth word in Scripture, if anyone is counting. It's when God said, "Let there be light…"[47] In the next chapter, I'll reveal why God speaks, referring to this verse. For now, I simply want to point out that God begins the human story by speaking out. He then commissions other prophetic voices throughout the Old and New Testaments to keep telling the story. The baton passes to us with the gift of prophecy made available to us all. You are invited to go and tell.

Being prophetic is…

The next six chapters will unpack the gift of prophecy. There will be stories, scriptures and practical tools to equip you. After this, the last chapter is then a final invitation to take up the gift. Before all that, I hope you will catch the heart and essence of what it looks like to be prophetic.

We've seen from Isaiah's experience that being prophetic is having a lifestyle of worship and encounter. It's recognising our

---

[46] *NAS Exhaustive Concordance;* Foundation Publication Inc (1997)
[47] Genesis 1:3

weaknesses and relying on His strength. It's also living in freedom.

If you can walk in these things, then the sending, the going and the telling will become naturally supernatural.

PART ONE

God's Voice

2
The Why

Our youngest child, who is our only daughter, recently blurted out on a family walk, "Dad, why did you have four children?" The question was clearly loaded with frustration towards her three older brothers, and to be fair, I am sure they were pushing the sibling boundaries (which they are experts at). However, my mind wandered, as I meanwhile utilised the classic parenting skill of ignoring the children and hoping the disagreements would resolve themselves. Why *did* we decide to have so many kids? What on earth were we thinking?

Unbeknownst to our daughter, in asking 'the why', she was fundamentally asking what the vision and motivation were behind our decision. Figuring out the 'why' is often a great way to start, particularly when exploring something for the first time or returning to something you may not have picked up for a while. So, after I got past my searching questions of why we had four kids, I reminded myself of our vision to have a big family and our heart to train our children to be Kingdom ambassadors and mighty warriors for God. It stirred me afresh for our family's future.

We will come on to the practical application and the spiritual activation of the prophetic gift later in the book, but don't skip ahead to the fun stuff because this first chapter is to answer the key, fundamental question of *why* God speaks.

"I speak because I can."

Let me start by telling you about the dream I had on Thursday, 20th October 2011. The dream was Manchester City beating Manchester United 6-1 at Old Trafford Football Ground. I know... shocking! As a third-generation Man United fan like me, this was more of a nightmare.

I remember seeing United player Wayne Rooney's face in the dream, looking distraught and in disbelief as the game unfolded. As I woke and smirked to myself at the thought of that result and the total unlikelihood, I got on with my day and forgot about it. No disrespect to Man City; it's just that Man United had a great 2010-11 campaign where they were Premier League champions for the nineteenth time and runners-up in the European Cup to Barcelona. You can't argue with facts! Besides, the loss was at home to United, so again, it was just unimaginable – another reason I shrugged the dream off and didn't give it another thought.

Three days later, on Sunday, 23rd October 2011, it's derby day! Man United is home to Man City, and I'm watching the game with friends – both blue and red supporters. To my sheer amazement, we begin to see one goal after another go in, and then, the final whistle blows as Man City win 6-1![48] It was unbelievable. The last time City beat United with five goals or more was in 1955 – so just unheard of. It was around the fourth goal that the dream I'd had on Wednesday night came to mind,

---

[48] bbc.co.uk/sport/football/15325536

and it dawned on me that it was from God and I knew what the result would be.

That Sunday afternoon, I was left puzzled. If I'm being honest, for a brief moment, I found myself trying to calculate how much money one would have made if they had placed a bet on those odds (I do not condone gambling; I was just intrigued)! That aside, I was puzzled, knowing God had spoken in a dream but not knowing why. I've had many prophetic dreams, and there was often clarity regarding what God was saying and who the word was for. However, I did not know why God had revealed this information to me in this instance.

I continued to ask God, into the following week, what the purpose of showing me this football result was. One thought was learning to listen better and not dismiss my thoughts, feelings and dreams as my own when it's actually His voice speaking. Another thought was to be bold to speak out. Imagine if I had prophesied this result before the match; it would have been scoffed at initially but would have proven to be incredibly accurate. So, learning to listen and being bold to speak out were both good conclusions and helpful with hearing God.

However, one morning, on my walk to work, I heard God simply whisper, "I spoke because I could."

God showed me the purpose of telling me the game's result was to reveal His heart for relationship and connection by speaking about the thing I am passionate about: football. He could have given me a result from any sport and team in the world, but He didn't. Instead, He spoke into my hobby and interest; though, of course, I would have preferred the result to have gone the other way!

God speaks for relationship

God took me back to basics and started to remind me that He speaks to us simply because He wants to. He enjoys talking to us, and it gives Him pleasure. Yes, He speaks with power and purpose, with all authority and with constant clarity. He speaks from heaven's perspective, which carries global ramifications as He holds the world in the palm of His hands.[49] He has an eternal and multi-generational voice as He sees the great tapestry of history, present and future. But do you know what? More than all that, He speaks to us because His desire for relationship pulsates out from His heart towards ours. It is not from obligation or requirement, but because His desire as a loving Father is to connect and communicate with His children. One of the greatest delights we have in our human relationships is the ability to communicate. That delight of communicating is designed and displayed by God. He longs to speak to us so that He may connect and relate with us as His sons and daughters.

We see God's heart for a relationship right at the beginning, in the first chapters of the Bible.[50] From a motivation of love and connection, He spoke life. In fact, our first recording of God's voice, His first four words, were, "Let there be light." God spoke the words of creative life because He could. God proceeded to speak, demonstrating the immense, awe-inspiring power of His voice as He built all of creation, including humanity, so He could communicate with us. In fact, the early

---

[49] Psalm 95:4
[50] Genesis 1-3

chapters of Scripture are littered with God demonstrating His intention to care, provide and connect with us. Mark Batterson says, "The voice of God is all-powerful, but that's only half the story. His voice is also all-loving."[51] From a place of deep love for us, we see this incredible design and

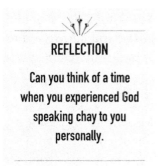

REFLECTION

Can you think of a time when you experienced God speaking chay to you personally.

display where God speaks life, creativity and expansion. God speaks for life and from love. These two relational themes can sum up the 'why' He speaks. Let's dig a little deeper.

He speaks for life

The Hebrew word for 'life' we see at the beginning of creation is *chay*.[52] This word has several meanings, including coming alive or giving vital energy to live. The same God that spoke *chay* at creation speaks *chay* into your existence and life's purpose.

Some years ago, noticing a couple in church that seemed unhappy and drew my attention, God gave me a word of 'vital energy' for them. I went over and explained that I felt they were carrying anxiety about not being able to conceive. Speaking life, I encouraged them that it was God's purpose for them to have a baby and then gave them some other specifics about the baby boy and his future. About a year later, new life entered their home as they welcomed their beautiful baby boy into the world.

---

[51] Mark Batterson; *Whisper;* Multnova (2017)
[52] 'Chay'; *Strong's Concordance,* 2416

Think for a moment about some of your unfulfilled dreams and goals, and allow God to speak life into them. If God can form you, this incredible person, by speaking life, then He can surely speak life into your destiny and make 'what is not' become a reality.

Moving from creation and further into Scripture, we see this theme emerging with God using His voice to speak life. Here's a great passage from Ezekiel 37:1-11:

> The hand of the LORD was on me, and he brought me out by the Spirit of the LORD and set me in the middle of a valley; it was full of bones. He led me back and forth among them, and I saw a great many bones on the floor of the valley, bones that were very dry. He asked me, "Son of man, can these bones live?" I said, "Sovereign LORD, you alone know." Then he said to me, "Prophesy to these bones and say to them, 'Dry bones, hear the word of the LORD! This is what the Sovereign LORD says to these bones: I will make breath enter you, and you will come to life. I will attach tendons to you and make flesh come upon you and cover you with skin; I will put breath in you, and you will come to life. Then you will know that I am the LORD.'" So I prophesied as I was commanded. And as I was prophesying, there was a noise, a rattling sound, and the bones came together, bone to bone. I looked, and tendons and flesh appeared on them and skin covered them, but there was no breath in them. Then he said to me, "Prophesy to the breath; prophesy, son of man, and say to it, 'This is what the Sovereign LORD says: Come, breath, from the four winds and breathe into these slain,

that they may live.'" So I prophesied as he commanded me, and breath entered them; they came to life and stood up on their feet—a vast army. Then he said to me: "Son of man, these bones are the people of Israel."

What a wonderful vision Ezekiel has! What's interesting is the Hebrew word for life here is *chayah*[53], which has a slightly different meaning to what we see at creation. Again, this word has several meanings: alive and kicking, revived and refreshed, or restored to health.

So, rather than new life being birthed, the emphasis here is bringing back to life. God's voice can bring back to life those things that have decayed. It's a voice of healing to your body, relationship restoration, divine provision, and resurrecting old dreams and aspirations.

Yes, it's a voice that can bring new life, but it's also a voice that helps sustain that life.

It reminds me of a coral reef documentary I watched. It is an incredible and intricate ecosystem, where each minute, living organism plays an important role in ensuring there is sustainable life for all. This is *chayah*. This is God's voice giving us continual sustainability with incredible intricacy yet with simplicity.

As we consider God speaking for life, we have *chay* (new life) and also *chayah* (continual life). Hold on to your seats as we explore the Greek in the New Testament, where we find the word *zoe*[54]. This is the word used by Jesus when He said, "I

---

[53] 'Chayah'; *Strong's Concordance*, 2421
[54] 'Zoe'; *Strong's Concordance*, 2222

have come that they may have life, and have it to the full." *Zoe* incorporates both Hebrew words. It simply means 'all-encompassing life'.

Jesus is the fulfilment of life itself. He is the fulfilment of all the Old Testament laws and prophecies, and becomes for us all-encompassing life.

Do you want to hear God's voice that speaks life? Look at creation for new life and consider passages like Ezekiel for continual life. Ultimately, though, go to Jesus, who will speak all-encompassing life.

A.W. Tozer says "the life is in the speaking words".[55] If you have areas in your life right now that feel hopeless, lost or dead, let me encourage you to invite God to speak creative, encouraging and faith-building life to you.

Driven by relationship and desire for connection with you, God's voice can pierce into your very point of need and bring you life. He can speak life into your marriage, finances and workplace; life to your children, neighbours and your city. There is life in His speaking words.

He speaks from love

The other biblical theme as to why God speaks for relationship is to communicate His love. I have already touched on how this unfolded in creation as God lovingly and lavishly provided man with everything he could ever need. Communicating and displaying His affection, God powerfully determined to place

---

[55] A.W. Tozer; *The Pursuit of God;* Christian Publications, Inc. (1982)

Adam at the centre of paradise. God's desire to reveal His love to us has been at the centre stage of humanity's story. Yes, there have been some troubling pathways and turbulent passageways throughout history, but God's intention for covenant love has always remained. When God speaks to us, His motivation is 'from love'. He is deeply and eternally committed to His relationship with us.

I mentioned the phrase 'covenant love'. Covenant is a significant word and not just in the Bible. My marriage to Rosy has covenantal implications that impact our relationship and family. I entered a long-term covenant with my mortgage provider, where both parties are committed to honouring the agreement throughout the contract term. Of course, a mortgage is a business relationship, while marriage is a deeper and more intimate relationship, but both are covenants I have made. It's important not to mix them up either. It would not go down well at all if I were to treat Rosy with a transactional, handshake-style demeanour. Likewise, our covenant relationship with God is not a handshake deal providing a service or access to heaven. It's an eternal commitment to a deep relationship.

God takes joy in speaking His covenant love over us.

Moses, speaking on behalf of God, explains it this way to the Israelites:

> …GOD wasn't attracted to you and didn't choose you because you were big and important—the fact is, there was almost nothing to you. He did it out of sheer love, keeping the promise he made to your ancestors. GOD stepped in and mightily bought you back out of that world of slavery, freed you from the iron grip of

Pharaoh king of Egypt. Know this: GOD, your God, is God indeed, a God you can depend upon. He keeps his covenant of loyal love with those who love him...[56]

The Hebrew word for 'covenant' here is *berith*[57], which is the most common. It means agreement, pledge, divine constitution and an alliance of friendship. I hope you are beginning to understand that when God speaks, it's not superficial or romantic love. He speaks from a love that is all-powerful and unwavering. He speaks with a deep commitment towards us. He isn't going anywhere and isn't changing focus. His face remains towards us, His heart beats for us and His commitment to our destiny is locked in for the long-term. Just as He promised the Israelites, God will also 'step in' at our point of need and speak His covenant to us.

We can't speak about love without mentioning Jesus. Just as God's all-encompassing life is found in Jesus, His all-powerful love is found in Him too.

Apostle Paul writes, "But God demonstrates his own love for us in this: While we were still sinners, Christ died for us."[58] God offering up His one and only Son as a sacrifice was the greatest demonstration of love towards mankind and ushered in a completely new era of covenant love in Jesus. This is where we can experience His love individually and personally. One of the reasons I love Paul's words is that they capture God's desire towards us in that He made the first move: "while we were still sinners". When I look back at my own life and consider some

---

[56] Deuteronomy 7:7-10 (MSG)
[57] 'Berith'; *Strong's Concordance,* 1285
[58] Romans 5:8

of the mess and mistakes, including the bad decisions and the bad words, I get goosebumps as I then consider the 'but': "But God demonstrated His own love towards us…" In that mess, God reached out His hand of grace and opened His mouth of love to demonstrate His unwavering, deeply committed,

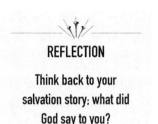

REFLECTION

Think back to your salvation story: what did God say to you?

eternal, passionate desire for a relationship with us. He makes the first move and says the first words. Why? Because when He speaks, it's 'from love'.

To truly understand this link between God's voice and His love for us, I highly recommend reading Shawn Bolz's book, *Translating God*. This book transformed how I hear His voice and use my voice in the context of God's love. Shawn says that the prophetic is one of the greatest tools of love that we have.[59]

Your voice from love

> If I have the gift of prophecy and can fathom all mysteries and all knowledge, and if I have a faith that can move mountains, but do not have love, I am nothing.[60]

After reading *Translating God* and being reminded of God's love, and linking that to the prophetic, I began to use this motivation 'from love' to hear God for others. You see, it's a win-win. First, our relationship with God deepens as our

---

[59] Shawn Bolz; *Translating God;* Icreate Productions (2015)
[60] 1 Corinthians 13:2

security grows in His love for us, and secondly, this love also spills over to those around us as we encourage others.

I started practising this and would look around the room at a Sunday service, spot someone and then consider just how much God loved them, cared for them and wanted the best for them. Then, as my thoughts and heart were filled with God's love for that person, He would give me glimpses into their life and future so that I could encourage them. As I got feedback, the spike in accuracy and sharpness went up a level. I was taken aback at how God speaking to us was so strongly motivated by His love.

It is also a brilliant evangelistic tool. On a family day out, while queuing for the dodgems with my son, a young staff member caught my eye, so I started to let my mind and heart capture God's love for him. Then, words about his future in politics, particularly within the European government, came into my heart. Bearing in mind I'm an introvert, sparking up conversations with strangers doesn't come naturally to me. However, motivated by God's love for this man, I went over and started a general conversation, showing interest and care. I didn't want to scare him off! I then gently explained that God loved him and had a plan for his life. I gave him some specifics of what I had heard. He allowed me to pray for him and was very appreciative that we had left our place in the queue to spend some time with him. (I am not sure if my son shared his appreciation!) So, let me encourage you to position your heart and mind to hear God's voice of love for yourself first and foremost, and as you walk in this, start doing the same for those around you. I believe you too will grow exponentially in hearing His voice and using yours.

Why does God speak? He speaks for the sake of relationship and does it for life and from love.

God speaks for purpose

Now, apart from relationship, another reason why God speaks is for purpose. Let's return to my nightmare dream of Man City beating Man United 6-1, and how God showed me that one purpose in his speaking was for relationship – that is, to speak into my passions and interests. A few months later, He shared a second purpose of the prophetic dream. I felt Him say that the game was representing a power shift in the city of Manchester. In other words, we would begin to see a shift in influence and power not just on the pitch but in the city too. Furthermore, the impact of Man City's growth as a football club would influence new areas of the city economically and socially. Interestingly, the BBC published an article on this game ten years on (22nd October 2021), in which Chris Bevan looked at the changes in the city over that decade. In his report, he stated, "That day signalled the start of a power shift."[61]

The prophet Isaiah uses the analogy of rain to help us understand the power of purpose:

> As the rain and the snow come down from heaven, and do not return to it without watering the earth and making it bud and flourish, so that it yields seed for the sower and bread for the eater, so is my word that goes out from my mouth: it will not return to me empty, but

---

[61] bbc.co.uk/sport/football/58995303

will accomplish what I desire and achieve the purpose for which I sent it.[62]

The purpose of rain plays a pretty significant role in the world's water cycle. If it does not fulfil its purpose of providing fresh water to the earth's ecosystem and all lifeforms, we will most likely die on an arid planet. In fact, it would be absurd for rain to fall and then rise back to the heavens without impacting the earth; there would be no point. It is exactly the same when God speaks. His words have a purpose – a divine assignment to fulfil and accomplish what God has purposed for them to do.

Knowing the purpose

We may not always know the intent of His words. Despite this, it doesn't mean they are not lining up with His purposes. It just means we may not see it. Whether we personally see His words come to pass or not, they will accomplish their purpose, or as Ern Baxter puts it, "If God has said He's going to do a certain thing, then … He will do it."[63]

In the Introduction, I talked about the four words I had heard, "Kings, Peterborough, Dave and Karen".[64] At first, we had absolutely no idea what the purpose of these words was, what they meant or even whom they were for. Because of this, we started our process by asking the 'why'. Asking this question from the outset set us on a healthy course of exploration. It opened the conversation, stirred faith and gave permission for process and pushing doors. After a time of working with those

---

[62] Isaiah 55:10-11

[63] Ern Baxter; *The King, the Kingdom and the Holy Spirit;* Destiny Image Publishers (1995)

[64] Introduction, p.15

words, it became crystal clear what
the purpose of the words was for us
and our next steps in the plans God
had for us.

It is crucial we know the difference
between purpose and outcome. His
purpose of speaking can vary, and it
isn't a case of His words achieving a
particular outcome, like a machine

REFLECTION

Take a prophetic word you
have received and spend
some time to think about
what the purpose is.

that, when switched on, sets off a chain of events resulting in a
finished product. For example, the purpose of Him speaking
might be to simply and tenderly allure us[65] or comfort us.[66]

I do not intend to give a comprehensive answer on the manifold
reasons and purposes of why God speaks, though I would
recommend you read Ephesians chapters 1-3 through the lens
of 'Why does God speak?' For now, here are two great passages
of Scripture:

> …he made known to us the mystery of his will according
> to his good pleasure, which he purposed in Christ, to be
> put into effect when the times reach their fulfilment – to
> bring unity to all things in heaven and on earth under
> Christ.[67]

> His intent was that now, through the church, the
> manifold wisdom of God should be made known to the
> rulers and authorities in the heavenly realms, according

---

[65] Hosea 2:14
[66] Isaiah 40:1
[67] Ephesians 1:9-10

to his eternal purpose that he accomplished in Christ Jesus our Lord.[68]

As you process the voice of God, these verses can be a bedrock for understanding His purposes. His intent is still being played out today "now, through the church", which means we have the opportunity to partner with God. As we hear His voice and use ours, we become part of fleshing out His purposes in our everyday lives, which is rather exciting!

Understanding the 'why' is a great place to start when considering the gift of prophecy, and helps us come to a biblical and revelatory understanding that God speaks for relationship and purpose. This sets us up nicely for chapter three, where we'll look at 'how' God speaks.

---

[68] Ephesians 3:10-11

Reflection and Activation

BIBLE REFERENCE SUMMARY

Genesis 1-3; Ezekiel 37:1-14; John 10:10; Deuteronomy 7:6-10; Romans 8:5; Isaiah 55:11; Ephesians 1:9-10; Ephesians 3:10-11.

SMALL GROUP DISCUSSION QUESTIONS

1. Describe why you think God speaks. What is God's motivation to speak to us?

2. How does God speak for 'new' life and 'continual' life (use Ezekiel 37:1-14 and John 10:10)? How does God speaking from love affect our relationship with Him (use Romans 8:5)?

3. Using Ephesians 1:9-10 and 3:10-11, discuss some aspects of God's purpose and how it relates to the prophetic. What are the connotations of "now, through the church"?

4. Are there any heart or mindset adjustments that can be made to deepen our understanding of 'why' He speaks?

MINISTRY AND ACTIVATION

1. *Pitch it* – a fun group activity. Get into smaller groups and prepare a two-minute pitch to give to the rest of the wider group. The topic is to promote your choice of fruit. Explain with passion and enthusiasm why you think the fruit is brilliant, why it is good for you and what the benefits are for consuming it! The point is that, similarly, when God speaks, it is to passionately communicate His love for us and remind us of our purpose and destiny.

2. *Prayer* – on your own or by getting into groups of two or three. Pray for a deeper experience and understanding of God's incredible love that motivates Him to speak words of life to us. Pray for a release of new and reviving words of life. Pray for God to break the power of words that haven't brought life.

3. *Bring a word of life* – on your own or by getting into groups of two or three. Take a moment of stillness to catch God's heart of love for someone else. Then, from that love, ask God for a word of life and encouragement to give them. In this safe place, share what you heard Him say. If you are on your own, ask God to show you whom it is for and share the word of life with them.

3
The How

Having started with the 'why', we now come to the 'how'. This reminds me of being a teenager and my longing to drive a car. I was desperate to get on the open road, embracing freedom and adventure behind the wheel. But I had to patiently pass both tests: the theory (I'm embarrassed to admit how many times I took this) and the practical (pleased to tell you I passed the first time). Not only did I need to know how to drive, but I also had to know how to maintain the car itself; which included knowing how to arrange the service, MOT and tax. I remember an attempt to make a repair myself, but only making it worse and having to reluctantly pay a mechanic to do a proper job. Eventually, I figured out the hard way that this freedom and adventure on the open road is very expensive! I had the 'why' but had to go through the processes of 'how'.

It is the same with hearing God; the 'how' is just as important.

No 'one size fits all'

There are so many ways God can and will communicate with us. Just look through Scripture and see how creative He is. He speaks through a donkey[69], a burning bush[70], angels[71], as well as dreams[72] and visions[73]. There is no one size that fits all, but a wonderful array of relational points of contact in which God connects and speaks with us on an individual and unique basis. I like how A.W. Tozer says that "[God] is, by nature, continuously articulate. He fills the world with His speaking voice."[74]

Discovering how He speaks is the exciting and exhilarating part. It's an invitation to lean in and listen. It is also an opportunity to develop our spiritual hearing.

Through a shop window

One of the earliest prophetic words I received was on my walk to a church service one Sunday morning. I glanced over at a charity shop window and saw a sign that read, "Get rid of your old clothes."

This phrase jumped out, not on a head level but at a heart level; something inside stirred with excitement. Thinking how strange this feeling was, and curious as to whether this was God trying to tell me something, I began to think through the spiritual meaning of the phrase. With a basic understanding of the Bible, my confidence grew as I considered that this could very well be God's voice.

---

[69] Numbers 22:28-30
[70] Exodus 3:2-4
[71] Matthew 1:20
[72] Daniel 7:1-14
[73] Acts 10:11-13
[74] A.W. Tozer; *The Pursuit of God;* Christina Publications Inc. (1982)

This was around the time I was grappling with the whole 'unqualified yet called' tension I talked about in the Foreword. I had a strong desire to be prophetic but was constantly held back by my lack of confidence, fear of failure and crippling doubt. I was also working through a mixed bag of identity issues of not feeling good or worthy enough for God to speak to me.

I arrived at the service with all this swirling around me. During the worship, this feeling that God was speaking grew to the point that I felt He wanted me to share this word with others. It may have looked like I was deeply engaged with worship, with my hands out and eyes closed, but internally, I was in turmoil! I had perspiration and palpitations while this battle of the mind and spirit ensued about whether I should share it or not! Finally, and in desperation, I said to God, "If this word is in fact from you, give me a scripture right now to confirm it and I promise I'll share it." In that very second, the scripture Zechariah 3:4 came to my mind! I promptly looked it up and, to my amazement, it read, "See, I have taken away your sin, and I will put fine garments on you." Before I knew it, my feet carried my body to the front of the service, and I brought along my first prophetic word to others. With a shaky voice, I encouraged the congregation that when God takes away our sins, it is like taking away old clothes and replacing them with fine garments of His love and grace.

It was by this very love and grace that, with all the insecurities and character issues I was working through, God set me up for an opportunity to hear His voice and use mine that Sunday morning. The 'how' was an everyday picture of a shop window

REFLECTION

Think back to how God speaks to you. Have you found patterns of similarity or maybe a variety over different seasons?

and the Bible. These ways, of course, developed, and others emerged over time as I cultivated my relationship with God.

Don't throw out the instructions

Understanding the 'how' is integral to hearing God and is not something to rush past. I'm confident I am not the only one who has opened up a new box of flat-packed furniture and just glanced at the instructions before casting them to one side and cracking on with the building project. Never a good plan, and in my case, it results in wonky furniture and leftover fixings.

A slightly bigger building project illustration is from my previous job as a Property Asset Manager. When an investor would roll out their vision to refurbish a block of apartments for the purpose of renting them out, my role was to make this happen. The investor had the 'why', and I would help form the 'how' through implementing a strategic plan. With no robust 'how', we would not achieve the 'why', and there would be half-refurbished apartment blocks across northwest England with no rental income!

If we skip past the 'how', throw out the instructions, and plunge ourselves into using our voice without first comprehending how God speaks, we may find, over time, the prophetic gifting in us experiencing stunted growth.

However, giving time to explore the 'how' will open up avenues and new possibilities for hearing God and actually nurture and enlarge the gift of prophecy in us.

The how gives confidence

We will go into Joseph's story in more detail in chapter seven, but for now, I want to make one observation.

He had two dreams about his future and his family's, which essentially told that a time would come when his brothers and family would bow down to him. As he described the dreams, there were a variety of responses. His brothers were angry and frustrated; his father rebuked him, and generally, there was a mix of negative emotions targeted towards Joseph.[75]

Interestingly, in all these varying responses, not one person doubted that the dreams were prophetic in nature. They may not have liked Joseph's interpretations – or his delivery, for that matter – but they seemed not to dispute that it was God speaking.

You see, Joseph and his brothers were familiar with God speaking through dreams. Their dad, Jacob, when he was younger, had had a prophetic dream about his future.[76] I imagine that Jacob's experience might have been a regular feature at story time with his children and grandchildren. The precedent had been set. The method was clear. Joseph grew up, and, just like his dad, God spoke to him through a dream too.

---

75   Genesis 37:5-11
76   Genesis 28:12-15

They had confidence that when God spoke to their family, one of the ways was through dreams.

In the same way, as you discover how God speaks to you, I believe your confidence will be cultivated, and your faith will flourish at the sound of His voice. Hearing Him will become sharper, and your response will become quicker.

How to hear His voice

Okay, without further ado, I want to share some ways God can speak to us. This is by no means exhaustive but simply an outline of some of the most common ways. As an aside, if you are new to hearing God, I would also recommend you consider the Alpha Course.[77] There is a whole session covering five ways to be guided by God. As we go through the following list, you may gravitate towards a particular one that affirms how He currently speaks to you. Let me also encourage you to be open to the promptings of the Spirit to lead you into new ways of hearing God too. In it all, don't limit yourself or God!

Scripture

All Scripture is God-breathed.[78]

Reading Scripture is the primary and the most important way we can hear God's voice. It carries God's authority and is filled with His promises to us. Because this is the main conduit of hearing God, it means we must read it! Some basic mathematics for you: the more we read it, the more we will hear Him!

---

[77] alpha.org/try-alpha
[78] 2 Timothy 3:16

Nicky Gumbel says that the main way God speaks to Him is through the Bible.[79] I am sure many of us will say the same. I love reading the Bible, and this whole area was a significant bedrock for my relationship with God and my development in the prophetic gift. Growing up in a Christian family, reading the Bible was not unfamiliar to me, but it was thanks to my youth leader that I saw a breakthrough. He would see my lack of confidence in using my voice to bring prophetic words and even pray out loud. He pulled me to one side and gave me a piece of advice that quite literally changed my life.

He explained that if I wanted to grow in confidence as to whether it was God speaking, then as a first step, I could look into Scripture, because it is God's word to us in written form. His advice was to simply put my confidence in the Bible. This straightforward guidance helped unlock hearing God's voice and using my voice with confidence.

It was reading Scripture that quietened the fears and insecurities that would often hold my voice captive. After speaking to my youth leader, I still remember at the next prayer meeting finding a psalm and literally praying this word by word – a great first step. I continued to use this model and then began to add a little 'freestyle' prayer based on the Scripture.

In the same way, whenever it felt like God was speaking, I would explore and study Scripture to confirm it was him. Many times, my prayer would be, "If this is from you, show me in the Bible." It's like the shop window story I shared. In this season of life, when my understanding of the Bible was limited, I would

---

[79] Nicky Gumbel; hope.alpha.org/listening-to-god-in-a-time-of-crisis

frequently get specific scripture references when I prayed this prayer. This was God's beautiful grace walking with me as my confidence grew and my knowledge of the Bible developed. (Getting scripture references like this is called 'words of knowledge', which you will see in 1 Corinthians 12:8.)

Now, I am not saying you need to quote scriptures line for line in every prayer and prophecy; the main thing is that the basis of the prophetic word lines up with Jesus as revealed through Scripture. You see, the Bible is not just our reference point but also our witness.[80] It carries God's ultimate authority and is what we can base our ultimate confidence on. Scripture can sometimes be taken out of context and twisted to prove an emphasis. So, having a good and well-rounded understanding of the Bible ensures that we keep His word in the proper context and do not isolate certain parts. In discovering His voice through the appropriate use of Scripture, Bill Johnson exhorts us to look at the person, life and redemptive work of Jesus as revealed in it.[81] To put it bluntly, any sense of hearing God that does not start and end with Jesus as revealed in Scripture isn't from God.

Scripture is first on the list of how God speaks because all the other ways should be confirmed through its lens.

Whether reading Scripture is new to you or you've read it cover to cover countless times, keep reading it. Do not see it as an optional extra, but as fundamental to your walk with God and the gift of prophecy.

---

[80] 1 John 5:9
[81] Bill Johnson; *Way of Life;* Destiny Image Publishers (2018)

There are so many resources available now with various apps, study plans and audio options. You can find what works for you. I am still grateful to the youth leader who gently pulled me to one side and pointed me to the Bible, which set me on a healthy course towards hearing God's voice and using mine. Be inspired afresh to discover your true identity in the written word of God and grow in confidence to increasingly hear His voice.

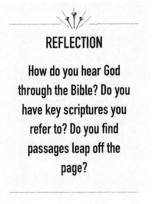

REFLECTION

How do you hear God through the Bible? Do you have key scriptures you refer to? Do you find passages leap off the page?

Small voice or whisper

Another way God speaks to us is through His still, small voice or a whisper. There is often the misconception that God uses a booming audible voice when, in fact, God's still, small voice is much more common. Duane White, Senior Leader of Bridge Church, talks about this in his 'School of Prophecy' training manual.[82] He explains that wrong perceptions can prevent us from hearing God's voice. He talks about how we can limit His voice to media and entertainment representations like Morgan Freeman's version of Evan Almighty, or we fixate on listening out for a thunderous audible voice when this is rarely the case at all. It was this small voice with which God spoke to us as a family that would redirect our lives into a new season. When He said, "Kings, Peterborough, Dave and Karen,"[83] the best

---

[82] Duane White; *School of Prophecy* (online training course)
[83] Introduction, p.15

way to describe hearing these words was like a whisper in my inner being.

Elijah had a similar experience when he was instructed to go to the mountain for God to speak to him:

> Then a great and powerful wind tore the mountains apart and shattered the rocks before the LORD, but the LORD was not in the wind. After the wind there was an earthquake, but the LORD was not in the earthquake. After the earthquake came a fire, but the LORD was not in the fire. And after the fire came a gentle whisper. When Elijah heard it, he pulled his cloak over his face and went out and stood at the mouth of the cave.[84]

It is easy to miss and even underestimate the power of God's whisper. Some ways to describe this small voice are a sense, an impression or a passing thought. God speaking through a whisper requires us to be alert and recognise His voice this way. However, it is also easy to mistake it for our own thoughts, so it requires active attentiveness and practice.

I wonder if God has spoken to you this way previously, but you have missed it or disregarded it as your own thinking? This 'how' can be developed by, for example, taking time to consider God's voice when a fleeting thought passes through your mind or an impression is felt on your heart. Like any new skill, the prompting to hear God in the whisper and then responding comes easier and quicker as we practise – much like learning to drive!

---

[84] 1 Kings 19:11-13

God will whisper words for us and those around us, be it a word that brings direction, instruction or a simple, loving word of encouragement and affirmation.

Other people

After God, the most significant other voice in my life is Rosy. Her voice, over the years, has had the most influence, whether I've liked it or not! It has brought me a hard-hitting challenge when I have not wanted to hear it and energy-giving encouragement when I've needed it. God will use other people to speak to you – at times, whether you would like to hear it or not!

We will come to the importance of the prophetic being embedded in community in the latter chapters. For now, I want to highlight that this is a vital 'how'. Apostle Paul was guided on his mission trips partly by God speaking through other people. Other people brought him words regarding whom he should take with him[85] and warnings about what was waiting for him in Jerusalem.[86]

Hearing God through other people usually happens in one of two ways. One is where someone purposefully shares something in their heart for you that they sense is from God. The other is where someone is talking more generally, and as they do, the words resonate in your spirit as something to pay attention to – a happy accident, as it were. Whether purposefully or accidentally, God will use both to communicate with you. Of course, we need discernment in both cases to

---

[85] Acts 13:2
[86] Acts 21:1-11

know it is from God. Again, we will come on to this soon. For now, though, be encouraged and alert to listen to other people's voices. It could be God using them as a vehicle to speak to you.

Dreams

Naturally speaking, our dreams are how our brains deal with the events of the day, a sort of cleaning and restoring of our mind and body. [87] On a spiritual level, our dreams are also where God can speak to us. Scripture is littered with God speaking in dreams[88] and clearly telling us that in the last days, our old men will dream dreams.[89] In the same way that not every thought is from God, not every dream is from God. So, how do we know when it is God speaking?

The first and most important test is to check that it aligns with Jesus as revealed in Scripture. From this, let me share two other practical tests (there are others, but these are most common) for hearing God through dreams:

1. REOCCURRING

This is where God will remind you of the essence of the word He is communicating through a dream. This could be in things like your Bible-reading, talking with someone or in prayer; something God will use to bring to remembrance the dream. This reoccurrence will act like a reminder to pay attention and further enquire from God what the word is or whom it is for.

---

[87]   psychologytoday.com/blog/why-do-we-dream
[88]   Genesis 37; Daniel 7; Matthew 2:13; Matthew 27:19
[89]   Joel 2:28

'Reoccurring' can also be in the form of having the same dream again. We saw this with Joseph in Genesis 37; the same also happened to Pharaoh later in Genesis 41.

God spoke to me in a dream about a church leader and that his season was changing from church leadership to education. Making a note of this word, I then left it alone. A few months later, Rosy bumped into this person's wife and discovered they were considering some changes without giving much detail. As Rosy relayed this conversation to me, I had a sudden reoccurrence of the dream from months earlier. This prompted me to give them a prophetic word which became confirmation for their next season.

2. WAKING DREAMS

This is when you wake suddenly, immediately after the dream; a sort of stark wake-up call. This could be waking up with alertness in the middle of the night with the dream feeling real. It also could be as you wake up at your usual time, but again, waking up with alertness and a fresh memory of the dream. The Bible often refers to someone being "troubled" upon waking from a prophetic dream.[90]

I dreamt that some close friends were having marital problems, though initially shaking it off because, from my knowledge, all seemed good and healthy with them. However, being woken up from the dream starkly in the middle of the night and feeling troubled for them, I began to recognise it was God speaking and a dream of warning. Contacting this couple confirmed that

---

[90] Genesis 41:8; Daniel 7:15

71

they were, in fact, having some serious marital problems, but – praise God! – they were able to be restored.

We will come to the appropriate interpretation of God's voice in chapter five, but for now, my encouragement is to let your prophetic dream life come alive!

Pictures and visions

Visions of the mind occur when the Lord 'projects' images and pictures onto the 'screen' of our imagination.[91]

It should not be surprising that God uses pictures and imagery to communicate with us; He is an expressive God. As humans, one of the fundamental parts of our language is the use of pictures; the first book you looked at would have been a picture book.

Pictures are deeply expressive and can paint a thousand words, whereas visions can be described as motion pictures. God delights in communicating His nature and love to us through the use of colours, patterns, shapes and such like. This is seen in Scripture[92] where God chooses to speak through images.

This 'how' is seen across generations, particularly with young people: "...young men will see visions."[93] When we give focus

---

[91] Kris Vallotton; *School of Prophets;* Chosen Books (2015)
[92] Ezekiel 1:1; Daniel 4:13; Acts 9:10 & Acts 10:3
[93] Joel 2:28

in our family time to hear God, it amazes me as our four children often share wonderful pictures from God. Some have been profoundly accurate. So, let me strongly encourage you to put time aside, maybe with your young people, to invite God to speak and then close your eyes and watch as He paints you a picture.

Creation

> The heavens declare the glory of God; the skies proclaim the work of his hands.[94]

David, in the Old Testament, beautifully communicates the heart of God. He expresses how God speaks through creation. The Passion Translation (TPT) paraphrases Psalm 19 like this:

> God's splendor is a tale that is told; his testament is written in the stars. Space itself speaks his story every day through the marvels of the heavens. His truth is on tour in the starry vault of the sky, showing his skill in creation's craftsmanship. Each day gushes out its message to the next, night with night whispering its knowledge to all.

Not only does the universe reveal something about the Creator, but it also contains a message for us. It's a loud and bold message, somehow shouting out to us. You could travel around the world, look up to the sky, and even search beyond into deep space, and something will speak to you of God's design, order and beauty. Paul writes that "since the creation of the world

---

[94] Psalm 19:1

God's invisible qualities—his eternal power and divine nature—have been clearly seen"[95].

The Bible is littered with creation metaphors acting as wonderful illustrations and imagery of God revealing Himself and His purposes to us. But beyond what is enclosed in Scripture, we can go out into it too! When we lived in Manchester, my practice would be to leave the big city and go to the hills of the Peak District to pray and hear God's voice in this awe-inspiring context. Moving to the flatlands of Cambridgeshire with no hills in sight, my new practice is woodland walks or one-night camping retreats where I can experience the night-time stars and the morning sights and sounds. I encourage you to get into creation and allow the surroundings to be channels of God's voice.

Whatever means necessary

When Rosy and I were getting to know each other as friends, and we both recognised that an emerging courtship could be forming, we were living in different cities at the time. We both desired to develop our relationship, but because of the distance, we had to figure out how. Such was our passion to communicate with one another rather than stick to one way, that as time passed, we ended up using whatever means were at our disposal! We would call each other, text (using actual buttons before the smartphone era!), email and even go as far as writing letters. For Rosy, it was like deciphering a coded message with my awful handwriting. We look back with fondness because, despite the obstacles to overcome, being

---

[95] Romans 1:20

creative in our communication grew our connection and developed our relationship.

In the same way, stirred by the passion for us and a determination to stay in connection with us, God will creatively use whatever means at His disposal to speak to us. He may be consistent in how He speaks to you or creative in showing you new ways. However He speaks to you, be expectant to hear His voice in increasing measure.

The 'how' puts flesh on the bones of 'why' God speaks and continues to reveal the fundamental truth that God is always speaking, which leads us nicely to our next chapter on learning to listen.

Reflection and Activation

BIBLE REFERENCE SUMMARY

2 Timothy 3:16; 1 Kings 19:11-13; Genesis 37; Ezekiel 1:1; Acts 2:17-18; Psalm 19:1-3; Romans 1:20.

SMALL GROUP DISCUSSION

1. Looking at how God speaks, why does He use different methods to communicate? Give some examples and draw from your own experiences.

2. When seeking to hear what God is saying, why is it important to take time to understand 'how' God speaks? What might we miss if we skip past the 'how'?

3. 2 Timothy 3:16 says all Scripture is God-breathed. Why is this an important truth to labour in the context of hearing His voice? Discuss this statement: "Any sense of hearing God that does not start and end with Jesus as revealed in Scripture isn't from God."

4. From the list (and maybe your own ways) of how God speaks, what is most common for you and what stands out as an area for development?

MINISTRY AND ACTIVATION

1. *Charades.* Get into teams and, using the rules from the classic game of Charades, try to communicate a figure from the Bible using only actions or drawing pictures. This fun game shows us that various ways of communication can be used, and God will also employ many ways to speak to us.

2. *Prayer.* In your own prayer time or in groups of two or three, begin by thanking God that He loves to communicate with us. Then pray for a new sharpness and measure, by His Spirit, in how He currently speaks to you. Also, pray for fresh faith for God to open your spiritual ears and eyes to begin hearing Him in new ways.

3. *Share a scripture.* Take a few moments to ask God to show you a Bible passage on your own or in a group setting. It might be that a specific scripture reference comes to mind, something you have recently read that stood out, or even a favourite passage you're drawn to for this exercise. Then share the scripture and what you feel God is saying through it. It could be a general word of encouragement, or maybe it is for someone specific. If you are in a group, share together and remember this is a safe place. So, be brave!

4

Listen Up

My dear brothers and sisters, take note of this: everyone should be quick to listen, slow to speak.[96]

Listening is important in any relationship. This includes a child listening to their parent as they attempt to communicate vital information for their own good and growth. Do they always listen? Not at all! Rosy and I have employed various strategies to deliver information in a way our own children would listen. This has become an increasing challenge now our older children have mobile phones. We are now in competition with even more voices!

The frustration of teaching our children to listen came to a head once when they were playing with their walkie-talkies. Instead of listening to the messages from the other end, they would constantly press the button and speak over each other. Therefore, only half-sentences and mixed messages came through! Overhearing this communication breakdown, I inevitably got involved and tried to teach them how to listen before pressing the button to speak, but this didn't work. I even went out and bought my own walkie-talkie to try to model how

---

[96] James 1:19

to listen correctly! I would use terms like "over" and "over and out" at the end of my messages to convey that I had finished talking and now they could speak. They just didn't get it and continued to speak over me, even jeering at my helpful teaching! Eventually, I gave up, and now my walkie-talkie just sits unused in my man drawer.

Who's got your focus?

Listening before you press the button to speak is not only a skill that requires development but also a discipline requiring focus. Unfortunately, our society landscape in this modern tech age is such that our lives are filled with record levels of noise pollution; the chattering of advertisements, opinions, 'breaking news', instant messaging… all voices contending for our attention. It can sometimes seem like a war as voices battle to grab our focus.

The UK advertising economy is one of the most sophisticated and dynamic in the world, and an average person can see between 6,000 and 10,000 adverts per day.[97] There are readily available statistics showing exponential year-on-year growth in the multi-billion-pound marketing industry.[98] In addition, social media platforms are also on the rise.[99] It is fantastic to see such a global connection, but instant messaging can also become a disruptive force with more unhealthy voices. Again, the growth of platforms like WhatsApp and Messenger over the

---

[97] www.thecreativeindustries.co.uk/industries/advertising/advertising-facts-and-figures

[98] https://ppcprotect.com/how-many-ads-do-we-see-a-day

[99] https://www.statista.com/markets/479/advertising-marketing

last two years has been staggering.[100] I love a good advert slogan or a funny GIF, like most, but at what point is it *too many* voices, and how do we ensure we're listening to the right ones? In all the hubbubs of the day, we need to learn how to tune in to God's voice and allow His voice to penetrate through the noise and distractions into our hearts and minds.

I heard a story of a young man who applied for a job as a Morse Code Operator. On arriving for his interview, he entered a large, noisy office with a telegraph clicking in the background. The young man completed his application form and sat down where seven other applicants were waiting. After a few minutes, he got up, went to the inner office door and walked right in. The other applicants were wondering what was happening. A few minutes later, the young man came out from the inner office where the interviewer announced, "The job has been filled by this young man." Grumbling, one of them spoke up, "Wait a minute – he was the last one to come in, and we never even got a chance to be interviewed. Yet he got the job. That's not fair!" The employer responded, "I'm sorry, but all the time you've been sitting here, the telegraph has been ticking out the following message in Morse Code: 'If you understand this message, then come right in. The job is yours.' None of you heard it or understood it. This young man did, so the job is his."

God is always speaking; the challenge is that often we're not listening. Have you ever found that the telegraph has been communicating, as it were, but you haven't managed to tune in to hear the message? Because of His wonderful grace and love,

---

[100] https://www.businessofapps.com/data/whatsapp-statistics

He will keep speaking. Not only that; if we invite Him to help us listen, God will show us how we can develop our listening ears. Having a voice is, of course, a key component of the prophetic. However, are we "learning to say things after listening to God, or saying things to try and make God's word fit in"[101]? Listening before speaking is twice as important; that's why we have two ears and one mouth. To develop in the prophetic, we must develop our listening.

Jesus listens

Jesus was a good listener to His Father, catching His heart and purposes:

> "For I did not speak on my own, but the Father who sent me commanded me to say all that I have spoken. I know that his command leads to eternal life. So whatever I say is just what the Father has told me to say."[102]

Throughout His ministry, Jesus was constantly surrounded by people, which would have created the challenge of regularly taking the time to listen to His Father. There were His disciples who travelled with Him; the crowds that would often form around Him; the haters who would follow and contest Him; the sinners He would seek out to show love and grace to; the sick that would be brought to Him for healing. That's a busy, people-focused schedule.

---

[101] Oswald Chambers; *My Utmost for His Highest;* Barbour Publishing (1934)
[102] John 12:49-50

It's interesting, then, that within this context, Jesus shows us that He considers carefully how He listens.[103] How did Jesus practically do this? Throughout the Gospels, we read that Jesus often withdrew to quiet, solitary places to pray and listen to the Father.[104] He was intentional about carving out time to listen, driven by an intimate and relational connection to His Father.

When it came to listening, Jesus was both intentional and relational.

Different approaches

Like Jesus, there is something about being intentional and relational when we listen to God. In our early days of marriage, Rosy and I came to recognise our different approaches to listening to Him. There was my intentional time set aside every morning, which was disciplined, rigid and, at times, slightly legalistic and duty-bound. Then there were Rosy's relational moments throughout the day, listening and interacting with God. I would sometimes look down on Rosy with my holier-than-thou judgements. Rosy's on-the-go relational listening was no match for my intentional 'God slot' listening! After repenting and experiencing a revelation of grace, I came to understand that, actually, it's a mixture of both.

Jesus' example to us is both. He shows us that effective listening is both intentional and relational; a beautiful tapestry of seeking out stillness to hear His voice, mixed with hearing Him in the spontaneity of the everyday. Let's explore these two principles a little deeper as we grow in listening to His voice.

---

[103] Luke 8:18
[104] Luke 6:12; Mark 1:35; Matthew 14:23

Intentional listening

Creating a dedicated space to listen to God's voice shows intentionality and priority. It places weight on God's voice over all the others. It's carving out time to find a sense of stillness and then using it to open our spiritual ears to hear.

REFLECTION

What's your experience of listening to God? Would your preference be towards the planned time or in the spontaneity?

Learning to listen intentionally is about developing the discipline to hear God. There is a commitment to say that no matter how busy life is or how loud the other voices are, I am determined to listen to His. We live in a hasty culture where stillness and serenity are lost art forms, and we find ourselves rushing about with activities, deadlines and projects. In the busyness, then, how do we cultivate the quiet way of life? How do we adjust the volume dials that would turn down the less important and turn up God's voice?

If we rearrange the letters of 'silent', we spell the word 'listen'! Perhaps we need to rearrange our schedules to discover the silence and improve our listening.

This is what Jesus did. He put time aside to intentionally listen early in the morning and late at night. He would dismiss the crowds and even the disciples while He made space, like up a mountain, to listen to His Father speak. Max Lucado says, "If we are to be just like Jesus, we must have regular time of talking to God and listening to his Word."[105] What does 'intentional listening' look like for you? It could be finding space in your

---

[105] Max Lucado; *A Heart Like Jesus;* Thomas Nelson (2002)

home or walking at a specific time of the day. Don't only create dedicated space to hear God but regularly "cultivate the spiritual discipline of silence"[106]. Finding a pattern of regularly spending time with God may not come easily, but by starting to prioritise it, we can actually train our brains. Being intentional regularly will form neurological pathways, which will become stronger with repetition until the behaviour is the new normal and listening to God will become a heightened experience.

Don't neglect the familiar

In the Introduction, I shared about hearing God give an important word for our future ("Kings, Peterborough, Dave and Karen").[107] This was a time when we felt a stirring that God was bringing a change to our lives but didn't know what that looked like. Part of this process included Rosy and me deciding that I would set some time aside to listen to and receive from God. After praying and receiving a prompting about a particular three-day Christian conference, we booked tickets with anticipation that God would minister and speak about our future. It was certainly a significant time away, meeting fantastic people, experiencing the Holy Spirit and further burning in me a passion for serving God. However, despite creating this extra space to listen and increasing my prayer time, God didn't give me any particular clarity about our future. I found myself returning home, having to make peace with it and trusting God nonetheless. The very next morning, after

---

[106] Dave Smith; *God's Plan for Your Wellbeing;* Waverley Abbey Resources (2020)
[107] Introduction, p.15

returning from the conference on 26th June 2019, God spoke very clearly and provided an answer about our future.

Funny, isn't it, that I invested time and money to listen to Him, and He chose to speak in my normal routine – at home, in my living room and in the morning stillness? God really does honour the faithful, intentional time we set aside to listen. Those regular moments we have with Him form a basis of connection where we can hear Him speak. There is nothing wrong with giving higher investment of resources to this endeavour, but nothing quite beats the regular and familiar routine and rhythms. So, don't neglect the regular and familiar discipline of listening.

Go into your room

"But when you pray, go into your room, close the door and pray to your Father, who is unseen."[108]

I like how this instruction from Jesus is super practical. Firstly, He tells us to go into our room. Considering the word 'go' is such a small word, it carries significant weight and packs a punch in the Bible. It is used 228 times in the English Bible and often used by God Himself in giving direction commands and linked to many of His promises.[109]

In this context of spending time with our heavenly Father, Jesus uses the word 'go' (or more literally 'enter') to inspire us to enter a physical space. This provides us with a very practical call to action. Jesus is encouraging us to purposefully leave where we are to intentionally go (enter) somewhere else for the

---

[108] Matthew 6:6
[109] Genesis 12:1-3; Matthew 28:19

specific reason of prayer. Jesus went, left where and whom He was with, to go and find a place to be with His Father. Let me encourage you to find your space and find your time.

Be specific: what time of the day? What room in the house (or elsewhere)? As you plan your time to 'go into the room', don't let it be an add-on to your day, where you try to squeeze it in somewhere, but rather let it be a priority. Personally, I prefer mornings, so my time spent praying and listening to God can set the day's agenda, atmosphere and tone.

Close the door

As we all go into the room, Jesus then very practically tells us to close the door. As mentioned at the start of this chapter, we can go into a space but still bring in distractions and other voices with us. Closing the door can silence those distractions and sharpen our focus in prayer and listening.

Even while writing this chapter, with my office door open, Rosy and the children burst into the house from their walk with a cacophony of noise and voices, which divides my attention, and I promptly get up from the desk and close the office door (after saying hello, of course!) As we consider our space for intentional listening, how can we each 'close our door'? It might be turning our phone off or sitting in silence and not filling the space with our own voice. It could be, more generally speaking, closing the door to certain voices that would attempt to fill our minds; for example, turning down the dials of television-watching or social-media-scrolling.

It could mean closing the door to negative voices around the work office or even the negative thoughts in our minds. So, let us each examine what particular doors of distraction require closing so that we might listen to the Father's voice more clearly than ever before.

When it comes to listening to God's voice, be intentional.

REFLECTION

Take a pause and note down what practical steps you can take to find your space to listen, and what doors you may need to close.

Relational listening

Jesus models for us that His motivation for listening was very much relational. His pursuit to listen was driven by His relationship with His Father. One of the biggest challenges and causes of relationship breakdown is poor communication, which is a failure to listen and take time to understand.[110] This is a growth area for me (honesty time) and something I have to work on in my marriage. If I am quick to speak and slow to listen, it does not go down well for our relationship!

We have already discovered that Jesus would retreat to have space to listen, but He would also have His channels of communication open as He went about His day, motivated by hearing the Father's heart for Himself and those around Him. Unlike my children, I am confident Jesus would have known how to correctly use the button on the walkie-talkie!

---

[110] www.relate.org.uk/relationship-help/help-relationships/communication

What is your motivation for listening to God? Often, we find ourselves seeking to listen to gain direction when we have a need or trying to find various answers. What if our motivation were simply for relationship, to draw close and hear His voice of love towards us? Let us take on the same example as Jesus and listen because we want a relationship.

Jesus spoke some of the most profound words the world has ever had the pleasure of hearing. He is still being quoted thousands of years later; countless books have been written to unpack and learn from His words. However, all the words Jesus spoke came from an overflow of listening and filling His heart with what concerned His Father, for the mouth speaks what the heart is full of.[111]

Listen like sheep

A great biblical illustration Jesus uses for relational listening is shepherding. He says:

> "The gatekeeper opens the gate for him, and the sheep listen to his voice. He calls his own sheep by name and leads them out ... his sheep follow him because they know his voice."[112]

As God comes close to us, relational listening is about truly knowing His voice. Way before the advances of today's voice recognition technology, Jesus, through the analogy of shepherding, shows us the depth of relationship we can have with God when we are able to recognise His voice.

---

[111] Matthew 12:34
[112] John 10:2-5

Sheep listening to the shepherd reminds me of the still, small voice or whisper in chapter three. This is one of my favourite ways God speaks because it oozes relationship and requires closeness and familiarity. Craig Groeschel makes the point that the reason God whispers is because He can. It is because He is so close to us.[113] I just love that our incredible Creator and Maker of the universe would come close enough to whisper words of life that would remind us of His great love towards us; what a great picture of a close relationship!

Rosy models this sheep/shepherd dynamic really well and helps me listen to His voice spontaneously. She would often say God had spoken to her while on the school walk, pottering around the house, or in the ebbs and flows of the day, like talking to a friend or close acquaintance. One afternoon in 2014, while Rosy was repotting a house plant into a larger pot, she felt God speak to her about us being repotted into a more spacious place. This soon led us, with guidance from our leaders, to doors opening and us taking on larger responsibilities in church life. This repotting brought about a growth in our leadership and stature and became the necessary stepping stone to where we are now. It was a beautiful relationship of God whispering words to His daughter in the context of the everyday.

Gift of love

Relational listening is fundamental to prophecy. 1 Corinthians 14:1 instructs us to follow the way of love and eagerly desire gifts of the Spirit, especially prophecy. The gift of prophecy is a gift of love and a means of relationship that has helped us to

---

[113] Craig Groeschel; www.life.church/media/god-with-us/in-the-wilderness

'follow the way of love'. Therefore, in our desire to grow in hearing His voice and using ours, we should begin by turning our hearts to Him and listening with the motivation for a relationship. We can then, of course, take this same model and prophesy from a place of love and relationship.

Acknowledge Him

"Here I am! I stand at the door and knock. If anyone hears my voice and opens the door, I will come in and eat with that person, and they with me."[114]

Once again, Jesus gets very practical about helping with relational listening. Firstly, there is something about acknowledging Him.

Years ago, I recognised an unhealthy struggle with unforgiveness in some of my relationships. So, I decided to receive some counselling to help in this area of unforgiveness. As my very helpful Christian counsellor began to help me navigate some pain and past hurts, she on one occasion advised that whenever I sensed an internal pain, negative emotion or bad memory, I should ask this question, "Where is Jesus in this?" Up to this point, I had seen my internal emotional pain as something for me to hide away, and I certainly had kept it separate from my relationship with Jesus. However, acknowledging that Jesus could actually be involved in this inner healing process was a revelation!

When Jesus looks at our life as a whole, our inner being, our daily interactions with others or the things we put our hands to, His heart is this: "Here I am! I stand at the door and knock."

---

[114] Revelation 3:20

Relational listening is about acknowledging that Jesus has such willingness and desire to knock on the door of all areas of our lives.

Listening to God in the everyday and the hubbub of life requires an acknowledgement that He is not only there with us but also wants to be involved. Jesus Himself constantly acknowledged His Father as He went about His earthly ministry, healing people and performing miracles. He said of Himself, "...the Son can do nothing by himself; he can do only what he sees his Father doing..."[115]

My encouragement to grow in our relational listening is to acknowledge God every day; to raise our awareness that He is present with us and wants to be a willing participant. For me, He was knocking on the door of my unforgiveness, though it took me a while to hear the knock. Once I acknowledged Him in this area, I was able to involve Jesus in my healing.

Invite Him

Acknowledging that Jesus is knocking at the door is a good, practical step. However, there is another practical step Jesus talks about in this verse regarding relational listening: we have to invite Him in. When my brothers and I were teenagers, we found it hilarious not to let each other into the house when one knocked at the front door. Instead, we would acknowledge their knocking but just ignore them as they stood out in the cold and became increasingly irate! It's one thing to hear the knock; it's another to open the door.

---

[115] John 5:19

As we invite God in to listen to His voice, He absolutely loves to speak into the seemingly insignificant parts of our lives, even our small decisions and interactions. Take a moment and think about your day or even week ahead: the busy work schedule, stressful meetings, lessons, studying or exams. You may also consider the mess and chaos parenting can bring, marriage or singleness, the difficult conversations with family members or friends, and the cyclical bad habits or patterns you perhaps have been battling. Jesus knocks at the door of all these scenarios and others that fill our lives. Will we then invite Him to come in and hear Him speak?

Peter Scazzero poses this healthy question: how can we cultivate the kind of relationship with God where the door is wide open?[116] One of our children recently started a new primary school and was struggling to make friends, which was getting him down and distracting him from his work. We advised him to ask people questions about their life. The next day, after school, he burst home with a beaming smile to tell me he had made a friend because he had asked questions and discovered that they had a similar interest! Asking questions is a beneficial way of inviting God in, like the question from my counsellor ("Where is Jesus in this?"). Slow down, take a breath and say, "Jesus, where are you in this?" and then allow Him to speak. This doesn't have to be at a tipping point or under challenging circumstances where you may need a particular solution. We can ask Him to speak into our everyday lives just because we want to hear His voice.

---

[116] Peter Scazzero; *Emotionally Healthy Leader;* Zondervan (2015)

I saw significant breakthroughs and freedom in forgiveness by opening the door to Jesus and inviting Him in. He spoke into the past pain and brought healing as I asked Him questions and learnt to listen to His voice in this area. More importantly, though, it brought our relationship closer, which is what it is all about!

REFLECTION

Is there an area in your life where Jesus could be knocking on the door? Give time to invite Him into that area and listen for His voice to speak directly into it.

A prophetic listener

A prophetic listener is willing to take the finger off the walkie-talkie button and, instead of talking, take the time to first of all listen.

Having had a minor health issue recently, and after researching online to read up on my problem, I decided it was time to visit the doctor. The doctors did their tests; meanwhile, I set about giving them the expertise and knowledge I had gained from my extensive online research (all of 30 minutes). Unfortunately, I was so caught up sharing my own self-diagnosis that I neglected to listen to them – the actual professional, qualified doctors. If I hadn't eventually been quiet and listened to their diagnosis, there could have been some unwanted repercussions! Listening first is not just life-giving, like listening to a doctor, but also empowers and stirs up the gift of prophecy.

We may live in the most inquisitive generation that has ever lived, but as we explore prophecy in each of our contexts and cultures, let us use the example of Jesus as we learn to listen; that is, each of us being 'intentional' and 'relational' listeners.

If it helps, try practising listening on a walkie-talkie; perhaps you will have more joy than I did with my parental teaching moment!

This concludes Part One, where we looked at 'God's Voice'. We have covered the 'why' and the 'how' God speaks and also examined the importance of listening. Part Two is all about using 'Your Voice'.

Reflection and Activation

BIBLE REFERENCE SUMMARY

James 1:19; Luke 6:12 and 8:18; John 12:49-50; Mark 1:35; Revelation 3:10; John 5:19; Matthew 12:34, 14:23 and 6:6; 1 Corinthians 14:1.

SMALL GROUP DISCUSSION

1. Can you give examples of where you have been quick to speak and slow to listen? How did it make the other person feel? What about the other way, when you were quick to listen? What were the differences?

2. What does Jesus mean when He said, "Be careful how you listen" (Luke 8:18)? How can we develop and grow our listening skills?

3. What does intentional listening look like to you? Share examples of how you currently put time aside to be with God. What is your sweet spot where you can find stillness (living room, particular walk, certain time of day, etc.)? Share what changes you feel could be made to 'close the door' (Matthew 6:6) to distractions.

4. What can be some of our motivations in listening to God? Discuss the importance of listening from relationship and how this could impact how we then speak. Remember, we have two ears and one mouth!

MINISTRY AND ACTIVATION

1. *Whose voice is it anyway?* – a group activity to show the importance of listening. This is where someone stands in the

middle of the room with their eyes closed. Each then takes it in turn to read a passage of Scripture, while the person in the middle tries to recognise their voice. You may have to change your voice to put them off by lowering your tone or putting on an accent. Likewise, we must develop our listening skills so that we can hear God's voice.

2. *Prayer.* Put your hands over your own ears, or in a group setting, get into twos or threes and put your hands over each other's ears. Pray and ask God to anoint our ears afresh to hear Him clearer than ever before. Pray that God would help show any adjustments needed to reposition and take time to listen to Him.

3. *Call to action.* From some of the practical 'calls to action' of 'intentional listening' and 'relational listening', decide what action you could take to increase your listening to God. Find someone you can be accountable to as we each together increase our listening to God and grow in our love and discipline of listening. Be sure to give feedback and ask each other questions.

PART TWO

Your Voice

5

Yes, You!

Have you ever found yourself doubting your own voice? Perhaps it has been just a fleeting thought that passes through the mind. "I don't speak confidently enough." "What if I get it wrong? Better to stay quiet." "My voice doesn't carry the authority others do." "What if what I say is rejected?" Have you experienced that in these examples, and so many more, you have simply concluded that it is easier to stay silent?

Let me start this chapter by writing this truth: you have a voice! Regardless of your age, race, personality, gender, past experiences, social status or family history, you have a voice. For some, you may not believe it right now, and for others, you may believe it but are unsure how to use or hone your voice. My heartfelt prayer and great hope are that we will each come to recognise we have a voice, and when it is used for God's purposes, it is truly a powerful voice!

This is me

There is a brilliant, behind-the-scenes video interview of Keala Settle, one of the main performers from the film *The Greatest*

Showman.[117] She and the film's director explained in this video that the cast had got together to play some of the film's songs in front of potential producers to see whether the film would get the green light to proceed into production. They go on to explain how terrified and nervous Keala was to have to sing one of the anthems of the film, 'This is me', in front of people for the first time, including film producers, no less. The video then switches from the interview to rough footage of her actually performing the song in a makeshift studio. You can visibly see the nerves as the music starts to play and Keala bravely opens her mouth.

She begins to use her voice to sing the song, and as confidence grows, so does her determination, passion and vigour, as she gives it her all. It is a wonderful visual of triumphantly overcoming her fears by deciding to go for it and sing at the top of her voice. It gives me goosebumps every time I see someone like Keala Settle, who, in the face of their insecurities and doubts, dares to use their voice and bring inspiration to those around them. Needless to say, the film got the green light! 'This is me' became a successful single in the global music charts,[118] went on to win a Golden Globe award,[119] and the film soundtrack remained at number one in the UK music album

---

[117] 'The Greatest Showman, behind the scenes with Keala Settle'; 20th Century Fox; www.youtube.com/watch?v=XLFEvHWD_NE

[118] en.wikipedia.org/wiki/This_Is_Me_(The_Greatest_Showman_song)

[119] www.goldenglobes.com/film/greatest-showman

charts for eleven consecutive weeks[120] and, of course, is played on repeat in our home by the kids (and parents!)

Your voice might not be destined to sing in films, but the truth is, God has given each of us the ability to speak. Julian Treasure, in his Ted Talk, says, "The human voice is the instrument we all play. It's probably the most powerful sound in the world."[121]

The question is, what will you do with your voice? It is always interesting when children start finding their voice, particularly when they use it in ways we would prefer they didn't: answering back cheekily, shouting at each other, showing their support for a different football team to me (most challenging of all). Our job as parents is not only to help them develop and discover their voice but to use it wisely and ultimately for the purposes of God.

Likewise, this chapter will set out to help you discover and develop your prophetic voice, and to do this, we will cover the meaning of prophecy and the 'gift of prophecy'. We'll also look at having a voice that carries truth and power. Finally, we will also explore how to use prophecy in the context of a healthy community.

---

[120] www.officialcharts.com/chart-news/the-greatest-showman-becomes-the-uk-s-longest-running-number-1-soundtrack-in-50-years__23169

[121] Julian Treasure; www.ted.com/talks/julian_treasure_how_to_speak_so_that _people_want_to_listen

What does prophecy mean?

Prophecy, taken from the New Testament Greek word *prophēteía*, means "speak forth", "make declarations by divine inspiration", "make predictions", "future foretelling", "asserting the mind of God" and "the gift of communicating and enforcing revealed truth".[122]

It is a spiritual communication from the realities of heaven that points us towards our divine destiny here on earth. Peter explains it like this:

> For prophecy never had its origin in the human will, but prophets, though human, spoke from God as they were carried along by the Holy Spirit.[123]

Or, in The Message translation, "Prophecy resulted when the Holy Spirit prompted men and women to speak God's Word."

From this verse, we see that prophecy is a revelation because it is God, by His Spirit, disclosing information about His heart and nature to us. More so, it is 'relational revelation' because the motivation behind God speaking is from love (like we saw in chapter two) and desire for relationship and partnership.

It's a gift

1 Corinthians 14:1 tells us to "eagerly desire the gifts of the Spirit, especially prophecy". This 'gift' of prophecy is different from the 'office' of a prophet in Ephesians 4:11, which is someone who carries a higher weight and authority within the ministry and calling of a prophet. The office is not for everyone,

---

[122] Strong's Concordance, 4394
[123] 2 Peter 1:21

whereas the gift of prophecy is available and relevant to us all. Here is a key scripture, 1 Corinthians 12:4-11:

> There are different kinds of gifts, but the same Spirit distributes them. There are different kinds of service, but the same Lord. There are different kinds of working, but in all of them and in everyone it is the same God at work. Now to each one the manifestation of the Spirit is given for the common good. To one there is given through the Spirit a message of wisdom, to another a message of knowledge by means of the same Spirit, to another faith by the same Spirit, to another gifts of healing by that one Spirit, to another miraculous powers, to another prophecy, to another distinguishing between spirits, to another speaking in different kinds of tongues, and to still another the interpretation of tongues. All these are the work of one and the same Spirit, and he distributes them to each one, just as he determines.

Here are three principles to understanding this gift of prophecy.

1. IT'S A GIFT OF GRACE

    We have different gifts, according to the grace given to each of us…[124]

It is not something we can attain through harder work or greater effort. Nor is it something that comes by striving to become a better version of ourselves. It is by God's grace,

---

[124] Romans 12:6a

through the Holy Spirit, that we can receive the gift of prophecy.

2. IT'S A GIFT OF FAITH

If your gift is prophesying, then prophesy in accordance with your faith...[125]

It requires faith to speak for God, and it is encouraging to know that "faith comes by hearing God"[126]. The more we hear, the more we believe, and then the more "we therefore speak"[127].

3. IT'S A GIFT OF LOVE

If I have the gift of prophecy and can fathom all mysteries and all knowledge ... but do not have love, I am nothing.[128]

In the same way God speaks 'from love', we are to do the same. Prophecy is a "love gift"[129] because it is designed to carry a relational connection towards God and each other. Therefore, it is not a matter of just passing information on in a robotic way like Amazon Alexa, but seeking to carry a heart and a voice of love. You see, it's not just words by themselves that will bring transformation; it is the love that underwrites them which carries the power.

One description of the gift of prophecy is, using our voice to speak God's truth through the love and power of the Holy

---

[125] Romans 12:6b
[126] Romans 10:17
[127] 2 Corinthians 4:13
[128] 1 Corinthians 12:2
[129] Shawn Bolz; *Translating God;* Icreate Productions (2015)

Spirit. Let me unpack what it looks like to have voices that carry truth and power.

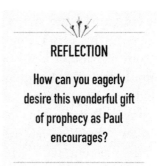

REFLECTION

How can you eagerly desire this wonderful gift of prophecy as Paul encourages?

A voice that carries truth

In discovering our God-given prophetic voice, we must understand that it is wrapped up in our identity as Christians and is part and parcel of who we are in God. When we become a Christian, and therefore a Kingdom ambassador, we become His mouthpiece here on earth.

Because of my insecurities about using my voice, I would try to resist opening my mouth by telling myself that speaking out was an optional extra to my Christianity, something that could be 'bought into' if I so inclined. In fact, our faith and our voice are inextricably linked. Paul puts it like this: "Since we have that same spirit of faith, we also believe and therefore speak."[130] As Christians, we can "dare to believe and then dare to speak"[131] into our own lives and the lives of those around us. "Prophecy in its purest form is speaking His truth."[132] By believing in Jesus, we can "therefore speak" truth with faith and assurance in our own voice.

God's heart is that every believer would use their voice that carries truth. We see this in the Old Testament with the story of Eldad and Medad, two elders in Numbers 11:24-30. They

---

[130] 2 Corinthians 4:13
[131] Smith Wigglesworth; published in the *Pentecostal Evangel;* March 30, 1940
[132] Duane White; *School of Prophecy* (online training course)

were part of the seventy that Moses hand-picked to take on some of his responsibilities. When the meeting was set away from the camp for this leadership transition, they didn't show up. Eldad and Medad remained in the camp while all the other elders were present at the meeting and experiencing an unprecedented ability to prophesy by the Holy Spirit. I don't know what they had booked on that day that was a priority over meeting with Moses and God Himself! The passage doesn't give much information, so I can only imagine that maybe they slept in, double-booked themselves or missed the Uber donkey! What's interesting is that even though they were not at the meeting, God still put His Spirit on them, and they began prophesying right there in the camp. This stirred up some indignation which caused Moses to respond by saying, "I wish that all the LORD's people were prophets and that the LORD would put his Spirit on them!"[133]

Moses' utterance to the people here and his heart's yearning became a prophetic statement in and of itself. We see it echoed through the Old Testament by prophets: "...and afterwards, I will pour out my Spirit on all people. Your sons and daughters will prophesy..."[134] We then see it unfold in the New Testament as the early church was filled with the Holy Spirit and the disciples started speaking out in faith.[135] Even today, we still see Moses' desire being lived out, as believers like you and me are filled with the Holy Spirit and given the ability to hear God's voice and use our voice to encourage those around us. Underline this: we all have the God-given invitation to speak

---

[133] Numbers 11:29
[134] Joel 2:28
[135] Acts 2:1-4, 14

the truth that can bring transformation – that includes Eldad, Medad and, yes, you!

Once, while discipling a teenage boy who had recently become a Christian, I was struck with the power of speaking the truth. For a time, we frequently met to talk about faith, the Bible and his identity in Christ as a new believer. This boy was into the 'gothic' look and wore all-black outfits, including jeans, a hoodie, a T-shirt, boots, a trilby hat and a long leather coat – all totally black! Personally, I had no problem with this choice of look, and we certainly turned heads when we walked through town together with completely different styles! However, I noticed he was masking some inner identity issues within this outer image. For example, he kept his head and shoulders sunk down under his hat and long coat, and often didn't make eye contact when talking to others.

Over our time together, I spoke truth into his identity rather than talking about his outer image, which wasn't really the issue. With a desire for his renewed heart and mind, I explained with scriptures that how one looked on the outside and spoke could display how one felt internally. I told him he had Jesus' light on the inside of him, and he was called to be a carrier of the Kingdom of Light to those around him.

Our meetings became less frequent, and a couple of months later, I walked past a group of teenagers talking together. Then, as I double-glanced, to my astonishment, there he was with a beaming smile and laughing with his friends. He wore a bright white T-shirt, light blue jeans and white trainers! I was just so astonished to see such outer transformational change in his life as he pursued the truth of who he was in Christ!

REFLECTION

Think back to times when you have used your voice to speak the truth in love. How did it make you feel? Consider any blockages that could be removed to prevent the truth that you have a voice.

Instead, speaking the truth in love, we will grow to become in every respect the mature body of him who is the head, that is, Christ.[136]

A voice that carries power

In Genesis 3:1-10, we see the first mention in Scripture of our voice carrying power. God had spoken to Adam and Eve with a clear direction for living in the Garden of Eden. Satan, in the form of a snake, came along and used his voice of temptation to lure them. Eve initially spoke up by actually repeating what God had told them:

> "We may eat fruit from the trees in the garden, but God did say, 'You must not eat fruit from the tree that is in the middle of the garden, and you must not touch it, or you will die.'"[137]

Relaying God's words to others is a great start for Eve and a powerful principle for the prophetic.

Unfortunately, Adam and Eve began to believe the snake's words and therefore doubted God's voice and theirs (which I am sure we all have done), and we see Adam and Eve fall into temptation and disobedience from God's garden rules. In turn,

---

[136] Ephesians 4:15
[137] Genesis 3:2-3

this causes them to go silent and hide, using their voices to speak fear and cast blame.

In it all, the passage shows us that even the enemy understands the power of our voice more than we do, and just like with Adam and Eve, he would actively work towards either silencing or controlling our voice. Do you realise that life, creativity and transforming power can come when you speak out on God's behalf? The enemy does.

I have a voice

I have only ever cried at the cinema once in my life, which was in 2011. This sounds unemotional, but I was just not much of a crier, certainly not back then, and especially not in public places! It was a surprise that the floodgates opened up while sitting in this large, dimly lit room surrounded by people. The film was *The King's Speech*. At the risk of further tears, let me explain. There is a scene where King George VI is increasingly getting frustrated and upset at his long-term speech impediment, and his mentor isn't letting up on challenging him. The discussion gets progressively heated until a moment when the king, through his awkward stutters, raises his voice and shouts with some gusto, "I have a voice!" These words, "I have a voice", continue to echo through Westminster Abbey and into the distance as the scene ends.[138] Meanwhile, here I am, in my cinema chair, face streaming with uncontainable tears. It was like those words had echoed off the screen and into my heart – *I have a voice.*

---

[138] 'The King's Speech {Official Film Trailer}'; www.youtube.com/watch?v=EcxBrTvLbBM

This stark reminder of the truth that I have a powerful voice was very encouraging and quietened all the doubts, anxieties and fears around my voice being unimportant and weak. It was sometimes quite confusing that I had this inner passion and a sense of calling to the prophetic, yet I was quite reluctant to speak up and did not enjoy using my voice, particularly in groups. My safe place was to gravitate towards the periphery, hiding at the back of the prayer meeting to avoid praying out loud or busy myself with serving 'behind the scenes'. It was like Saul, who hid among the bags when he had heard God's calling to be king[139], or like Jonah, who ran away on a boat after hearing God's voice for a city.[140] We can also compare it to Gideon reluctantly stepping up to lead the people even after hearing God's word and confirmation.[141] I gave myself such a hard time for not speaking up.

Part of this process was developing my confidence on a natural level, but there was also a spiritual dynamic at work. I came to recognise that we have an enemy, Satan, who relishes the opportunity to feed any fear of speaking out, reminds us of our failures and uses his tactics to try to keep us silent. It can become a spiritual battle for who would have the last word.

The apostle Paul writes:

> My message and my preaching were not with wise and persuasive words, but with a demonstration of the Spirit's power.[142]

---

[139] 1 Samuel 10:22
[140] Jonah 1:3
[141] Judges 6:11
[142] 1 Corinthians 2:4

Our words can come with a demonstration of the Spirit's power that can be both weapons to defeat the spiritual enemy and tools to advance the Kingdom of Light. So, when we use our voice to encourage work colleagues, give hope to the stranger at the supermarket checkout, use words of life at mid-week small group and so many

REFLECTION

Set a challenge to bring an encouraging word to someone, perhaps using your voice in a new setting.

more ways, we are releasing words that will destroy the enemy and bring purpose and hope into people's hearts.

Our voice will build people up into their destiny, grow their identity in Christ and cause exhilarating life to come into existence; now, that's powerful stuff! So, don't be silent. Speak up and use your powerful, prophetic voice!

Your voice in a healthy community

One of the most fantastic things about the prophetic is that it is a community venture. It's a team sport. Yes, you as an individual have a unique voice. However, we need to operate in the gift of prophecy within the safety and context of a community of believers. God speaks to 'us', not 'me'.

It's within this church community that a prophetic culture can flourish, where everyone has something to contribute[143] and we can together test and weigh the words and respond accordingly. Prophesying in a community is a biblical concept evident in the

---

[143] 1 Corinthians 14:26

Old Testament[144] and then in the early church, where one key example is with the church in Corinth. I encourage you to read the full chapter of 1 Corinthians 14. Paul encourages the church to pursue the gift of prophecy; in particular, giving some clear instructions for doing it in a good community: "Two or three prophets should speak, and the others should weigh carefully what is said."[145]

When Rosy and I received a word from God about "Kings, Peterborough, Dave and Karen",[146] we quite literally had no idea what this meant. As we prayed and processed this word, we recognised the need to find people to help us in the process. (Note: it is crucial to find people to talk with *in* the process, not *at the end of* the process when decisions may have already been formed.) We asked our leaders in Manchester and some intercessory friends, and also connected with the leaders in Peterborough. Processing with a small, trusted community was incredibly insightful and helped us see that God was calling us to the wonderful city of Peterborough!

In fact, I would like to suggest that, for the most part, a healthy community of believers should be the only way we use our prophetic voice. Here are two reasons.

1. COMMUNITY GIVES ACCOUNTABILITY

Guess what? We will all get it wrong at one time or another. Giving a word to someone comes with risks. It requires faith, boldness and vulnerability. We are all susceptible to blinkered

---

[144] Numbers 11; 1 Samuel 10:11
[145] 1 Corinthians 14:29
[146] Introduction, p.15

perspectives and blind spots. It can get a little messy sometimes, and mistakes can be made. While we are eagerly desiring to prophesy, surrounding ourselves with people of love and grace will provide a support network of openness, correction and encouragement. This kind of accountability requires humility, but it is the rich soil in which the prophetic gift can develop and grow.

Remember, prophecy is a grace gift, which means it is possible to operate in the gift while your character is still maturing. So, being connected to trusted people can actually be a discipleship opportunity. It could be that you check with someone trusted to help process it before giving a particular word. Or you speak to the person afterward so you can weigh the word together. It's also helpful to keep a journal of the words so you can look back and track them. It is a good idea to find a mentor who can give one-to-one accountability.

On 4th March 2015, God gave me a word that there would be a shift in the political arena. He said this shift would disrupt our nation, but not to worry, He is on the throne and was preparing His people for a season that would be shaky. This felt like a heavy word, so I shared it with my senior church leaders for accountability, and they helped weigh the word together to find the best way to process it.

Just over a year later, on Thursday, 23rd June 2016, the UK voted to leave the European Union. I remember looking around our Sunday service that weekend and sensing tension and some anxiety among our congregation, who were processing what had just happened. However, I also remember our senior leader standing up to speak and pray for peace over us and continuing to steady the ship and navigate our community through the initial shifting change in the political arena. Because of good prophetic accountability and support, we could carry this word together and respond effectively.

2. COMMUNITY GIVES RELATIONSHIP

At its core, the prophetic gift is a relational gift. "It is not a one-way communication"[147] but requires multiple parties. It brings people together and is not designed to be worked out in isolation. It is a dynamic team in which we all get to participate in whatever position we are 'on the pitch'. The Bible says, "For we know in part and we prophesy in part…"[148] You can bring your part of the word and allow others to bring theirs; together, we hear His voice and use ours.

When we all use our voices, there is this rich, stunning sound of diversity and inclusivity that delights God's heart of unity – just beautiful! It is also a multi-generational prophetic community. For example, in our family prayer times, we sometimes take turns to go in the middle and bring each other words. Our children have brought some simple yet powerful words to each other (a lot in picture form, as mentioned in chapter three). This encourages each of us and, more importantly, deepens our relationships. One of my greatest breakthroughs in the prophetic gift was when my youth leader pulled me to one side (again, see chapter three) to encourage and instruct me in using my voice (to speak out Scripture). The key was in how he shared his advice: not in frustration, but in relationship and love toward me.

---

[147] Bill Johnson; *Way of Life;* Destiny Image Publishers (2018)
[148] 1 Corinthians 13:9

I have a voice

What will you do with your voice? What practical steps could you take to help grow your belief in using your voice for God's purposes? My prayer is for you to have a fresh revelation that you indeed have a powerful and prophetic voice when used for God. Let me encourage you to eagerly desire the gift of prophecy and do this in a healthy community of believers. The next chapter will look at some of the practicalities and processes for using this wonderful gift. In the meantime, why not watch *The King's Speech;* then afterwards, find a mirror and declare over yourself, "I have a voice!"

Reflection and Activation

BIBLE REFERENCE SUMMARY

1 Corinthians 14; 1 Corinthians 13:9; Romans 10:17 and 12:6;
2 Corinthians 4:13; 1 Corinthians 12:4-11, 26; Ephesians 4:15;
Numbers 11:24-30; Genesis 3:2-12; 2 Peter 1:21.

SMALL GROUP DISCUSSION

1. Give examples from your experience where you have found
   yourself doubting your own voice. Conversely, give
   examples of when you have been inspired by other voices
   that have spoken positively.

2. What comes to mind when you think of 'prophecy'? Why is
   prophecy revelation? (Use 2 Peter 1:21.)

3. Reading 1 Corinthians 12:4-11 and 1 Corinthians 14:1,
   what stands out for you when you consider the gift of
   prophecy? What practical steps can you take to eagerly
   desire the gift?

4. Describe what you think a healthy prophetic community
   looks like. Within this, why are accountability and
   relationship so crucial?

MINISTRY AND ACTIVATION

1. *When is my birthday?* A fun group activity to illustrate
   prophetic community is to go around the room and try to
   guess each other's birthday day and month. It is likely that
   most would guess incorrectly. The point is, we do
   sometimes get it wrong, but that's okay because we are in a
   loving, supportive community.

2. *Prayer.* Create a space for some worship time where you can focus on God and invite the Holy Spirit to present Himself. If you are in a group setting, allow those that want to receive the gift of prophecy, or grow in it, to be prayed for. Lay hands on them (if appropriate) as you pray ("I remind you to fan into flame the gift of God, which is in you through the laying on of my hands." – 2 Timothy 1:6). If you are on your own, pray to God, by His grace, to impart the gift of prophecy to you or stir it in you afresh. Pray for an increase of faith to receive and participate in it.

3. *Call to action.* Choose one or two partners that can become your healthy community. Commit to holding each other accountable – maybe to even bring a word of encouragement to someone this coming week. Share testimonies and things you have learnt from the exercise. Then go again the week after!

6

In Practice

> Beginning to practice this gift is where the rubber meets the road — and where we encounter our fears ... but don't let fear of enduring the growing process stop you from moving forward ... I have found it is worth the effort.[149]

One of my favourite birthday presents as a teenager was a toolbox. That's right, upon request and probably to stop me constantly 'borrowing' my dad's tools, my parents got me a little toolbox with some basic tools. I loved my toolbox and would set about offering to do repairs around the house, 'fixing' things with my hammer! I've always been hands-on. It was around this time I tried to change my bedroom light fitting and blew the house electrics. My parents weren't very pleased about paying an electrician for an emergency callout, but at least I was able to observe him for next time's sake. Though, in my parent's home, there was no next time!

I like the fact that prophecy is very practical. The gift of prophecy is like a tool in our toolbox because it requires some practical guidance and application for correct use (like how not

---

[149] Jon Bloom, contributor for John Piper's ministry; 'Desiring God'; https://www.desiringgod.org/articles/prophecy-for-beginners

to change a light fitting!) We can study the scriptures concerning prophecy, which is, of course, important, but we must get our hands on and practise what it looks like to hear His voice and use ours.

Practice doesn't come overnight. We were born without ever using our voice, yet it was in our nature and design to start trying to use it. You have been practising using your voice since you were born. In the early years, it would have been as simple as imitating the sounds you heard around you. In fact, research shows the more words a baby hears, the faster they learn to talk.[150] The same principle applies to the prophetic. The more you practise, the greater the measure and development.

We've already looked at 1 Corinthians 14 (in chapter five) where Paul lays out some very practical instructions to the church for using the prophetic gift. The passage shows that as the Corinthian church community practised prophecy, there followed confusion and chaos.[151] Paul writes about using intelligible words, timing and sequence, and practising in a fitting and orderly way. In it all, I see a picture of a healthy 'give it a go' culture, and it certainly makes for an interesting, vibrant church community.

Using 1 Corinthians 14 as our framework, I will unpack some practices to equip you to prophesy at a higher level.

---

[150] 'How a baby learns to talk';
www.webmd.com/parenting/baby/baby-talk
[151] 1 Corinthians 14: 9, 31, 40

It's a community project

Though I've highlighted this already in chapter five, I want to underline the importance of community. In the practice of giving and receiving prophecy, the process should be within the context and safety of a community of believers where we are accountable and in relationship with others.

As a teenager, while visiting Leicester, a church leader with whom I did not have a strong relationship gave me a directional, prophetic word: I would no longer live in the north of England. There was no conversation or checkup afterwards, just an isolated word. This brought me a great deal of confusion and anxiety at a stage of life when I was exploring what my future might look like. This leader should not have prophesied in this way: isolated and unchecked. It was only when I brought the word inside the community by sharing it with trusted friends and leaders, and we weighed it together, that I recognised it was not from God.

The Message translation puts this really well:

> Then each speaker gets a chance to say something special from God, and you all learn from each other. If you choose to speak, you're also responsible for how and when you speak.[152]

As we practise this wonderful gift, we are all learning from each other and processing together. Let me encourage you to find your community to whom you can be responsible for how and when you speak.

---

[152] 1 Corinthians 14:29 (MSG)

Giving and receiving

Remember, the goal of giving and receiving prophetic words is relationship. It is to ensure there is an invitation to draw us closer to God and each other. This should flow through every word you give or receive.

When giving a word, if you sense it has the potential for confusion or anxiety, perhaps process it with trusted people beforehand. Rosy and I often prayerfully consider together before giving a word that could be direct for someone. We would process what we sense could be the best way to communicate it (i.e. phone, face-to-face, both go together) and also when to give it (i.e. whether it is something to hold and wait). This is really helpful as we process the 'how and when we speak'.

When receiving a word, it is also essential to process it well. Maybe you can relate to receiving an isolated prophetic word that brought confusion or anxiety. Though it may be deeply personal, please take time to process it, particularly with those you can confidently trust to weigh, explore and process it together. Also, does it line up with other words you have received and, of course, through Scripture as revealed in Jesus?

REFLECTION

Do you have a practical process in place for giving words to others and for receiving words from others? Take some time to form new or amend existing practices.

Purpose of prophecy

In the Old Testament, prophecy generally came from people God would set aside as His mouthpieces on earth. They would be anointed by the Spirit to specifically fulfil the role of the prophet.[153] As we enter the New Testament, we see the principle and, subsequently, the purpose of prophecy shift and evolve. Through the promised outpouring and the infilling of the Spirit,[154] prophecy is no longer restricted but available as a gift to each of us.[155]

Paul gives us three specific purposes for New Testament prophecy: "But the one who prophesies speaks to people for their strengthening, encouraging and comfort."[156] So, let's unpack them a little.

1. STRENGTHENING

(NASB: "edification"; ESV: "upbuilding")

Bringing someone a prophetic word should always be to build up and never to tear down. Working in the property industry for twenty years, I have seen first-hand how important it is to build and construct something well and the detrimental damage when it is not done! Building someone up in love[157] can be done by using words; that is to 'pull out the gold' in them and speak the truth that would enable them to see their destiny and purposes in God.

Imagine a prophetic word as a brick that will be skilfully placed on the other bricks of someone's life, which, when done well, will add strength and stability. That's the goal! The last thing

---

[153] Jeremiah 1:5; Isaiah 6:9; Ezekiel 2:1-7
[154] Joel 2:28
[155] Acts 2:4
[156] 1 Corinthians 14:3
[157] Ephesians 4:16

we want to do is speak words that would bring anxiety, fear or worry, which could cause cracks and splinters. Have you ever come away from receiving a word and it felt as if you have just had a life-energising boost? Like you have just had a strength workout on the weights? This is the power of prophecy at work, as it brings strength. In the same way, let strength be an underlining purpose as you prophesy.

2. ENCOURAGING

(NASB: "exhortation"; ESV: "encourages")

The dictionary definition of encouragement is "to give someone courage" and "to inspire courage"[158]. A significant purpose of prophecy is to impart hope, courage and insight into people's lives that would encourage them to fulfil their God-given destinies.

A prophetic word should inspire hope that causes people to continue, persevere even in tough times and keep running their race. We see this purpose of encouragement at work through the New Testament: "Judas and Silas, who themselves were prophets, said much to encourage and strengthen the believers."[159]

There is often a misconception that it's doom and gloom when it comes to prophesying – not so true! Prophetic people should be the most encouraging people on earth. "This is not to say that every encouraging sentiment is prophetic, but every prophecy should definitely be encouraging."[160] If you have

---

[158] 'Encourage' definition; dictionary.com/browse/encourage
[159] Acts 12:32
[160] Kris Vallotton; *School of Prophets;* Chosen Books (2015)

found that your prophetic process, in terms of delivery or content, hasn't been particularly encouraging, please don't be discouraged. Instead, take some reflective time and ask God and others to show you how you could make some adjustments so that you can bring words that inspire hope and courage in others.

3. COMFORT

(NASB: "consolation"; ESV: "consolation")

The third principle from Paul is bringing prophetic words of reassurance and comfort. This is a little more specific and would tend to be in times of despair or hardship. It carries God's fatherly heart of compassion for people and speaks into their lives from that position and heart. I would also link kindness to comfort as well ("So the Lord spoke kind and comforting words..." – Zechariah 1:13). A word of comfort said in kindness has the power to springboard someone out of a difficult season and into fresh hope and purpose.

It is a word where delivery is important and requires a soft, tender-hearted voice, not a booming loud tone. There is a reason Paul includes comfort in this list of prophesying well, so please, do not underestimate or dismiss such comforting words as less powerful or impactful.

Let these three purposes from Paul act as an internal check when you prophesy. Is the word going to build and strengthen the person receiving the word up into their destiny? Is it going to inspire courage so that they can continue? Will it be a kind and comforting word in tone and content?

Developing the gift

I am sure you are picking up that developing the prophetic gift is a process. There are layers and measures to journey through and learn. However, committing to your development is integral to hearing God's voice and using yours.

This hit home several years ago when I attended a fantastic conference with some good friends in July 2014. The conference was in Harrogate, England, where Bill Johnson and Kris Vallotton were the main speakers. In one of the evening worship sessions, I heard the Holy Spirit whisper in my spirit, "In five years, I am going to take you from tens to thousands." This took me aback because receiving personal and directional words are rare for me. While processing this word, my imagination got a little carried away. I pictured myself returning to the same conference in five years and being on stage, in front of the "thousands", retelling this story! I even went one step further and imagined myself on a mega international platform, speaking to multitudes. After snapping out of my over-imaginative thought-life and praying for humility(!), I began the journey of trying to work out what this word meant. How was I going to go from our current situation, which was part of the leadership in a church campus of approximately thirty people, to the thousands?

Rather than fixating and dreaming of the conclusion in five years' time, which was actually becoming a distraction, I instead decided to put my focus on the day ahead. That was to be intentionally present on that day and look around to whom I could bring an encouraging word. So, I took my focus off the "five years" and the "thousands" and instead faithfully and steadily developed my prophetic voice and personal character in what was right in front of me.

Fast forward five years to June 2019, and I had forgotten about this word. However, God gave us the next piece of the story: "Kings, Peterborough, Dave and Karen."[161] You know this story by now! We are currently settled in Peterborough, where I work for a wonderful church community and have the privilege of helping see lives transformed and discipled numbering into the thousands.

> ### REFLECTION
>
> **What step can you make today to develop the gift? Perhaps take this opportunity to look back at the Voice Check Assessment on pages 14–17.**

Please, hear me when I say it is not about the numbers or the timeline; not at all. The point is this: to grow in the prophetic, begin the process now! Don't wait for someone else, a better environment or a more comfortable season. Instead, faithfully steward your God-given voice and allow the process to develop and grow. Whether prophecy is a new area for you, or you are a seasoned operator in the 'gift, the exhilarating truth is that there can be more to unpack when we give ourselves to the practice.

Practicalities of prophecy

For some reason, many people think prophets should be able to bypass the practice and skill-building process ...

---

[161] Introduction, p.15

we expect people to prophecy as experts in their early seasons, but it just never happens that way.[162]

We're going to get super practical now. You see, I think practising prophecy is not too dissimilar to practising a sport or hobby. Let's take fishing, for example. Now, I hate fishing; sorry if this offends you! But believe me, I have attempted it on several occasions, including once with my brother-in-law, who graciously took me through all the practicalities of fishing. Also, at another time, I took my son, which was very much the blind leading the blind. Fishing is very technical and intricate and is a skill that requires much practice. It also involves a lot of patience, something I possess little of!

Having said that, my dislike somewhat softened when I noticed that prophecy is a bit like fishing. Proverbs 20:5 says, "The purposes of a person's heart are deep waters, but one who has insight draws them out."

'One who has insight' is a great description of someone functioning in the prophetic gift. A primary role of the gift is to skilfully and carefully 'cast out' our words into the deep waters of a person's heart and draw up their purposes and destiny to the surface. This takes patience, process and, of course, like fishing, it takes practice. You have to give it a go.

These following practical tips have been gathered from many years of process and practice and are by no means exhaustive. They particularly draw on mistakes made, experiences gleaned, mentors who have guided me in them and, of course, the Bible. My hope is that they can help us carefully and skilfully draw

---

[162] Shawn Bolz; *Translating God;* iCreate Productions (2015)

up people's purposes from the deep waters of their hearts that will help propel them into their God-given destinies.

Speaking with faith

In chapter two, we covered the importance of speaking words of life. Remember Ezekiel's vision, "So I prophesied as he commanded me, and breath entered them; they came to life and stood up on their feet – a vast army."[163] Prophecy has the power to speak 'new life' into existence and 'refreshing life' that brings restoration. It requires faith to speak prophetic life into people's situations, businesses, communities and cities. It is not a passive faith but an active faith that can mature.

If you want to develop the gift of prophecy, start by developing your faith. We believe, therefore we speak.[164] So, it is vital that in our personal walk with God, we not only maintain a level and a posture of faith but also look to stretch and expand our faith.

Some years ago, when asking God for an increase in the sharpness of hearing His voice, I felt a conviction to increase my faith. God showed me the need to raise my faith in order to raise my gifting. So, I gave some focus to growing my personal faith with things like Bible studies on faith and characters of faith, reading faith-related books and increased my prayer time, asking for more faith. At that time, I was at my friend's home, who was desperate to sell their house to improve their circumstances. It had been on the market for a while, but without any strong leads. I sensed God saying, "Here is an

---

[163] Ezekiel 37:10
[164] 2 Corinthians 4:13

opportunity to now prophesy life in line with your faith." I declared that they would receive an offer that weekend (this was on a Thursday). They got a last-minute viewing on Friday and received an offer thatt Saturday, and were able to complete the move soon after.

For us to be ready and available to speak life-giving prophetic words as God commands, it must come from an overflow of personal faith life. There are many practical ways to grow our faith; I encourage you to be led by God and give your faith some focus.

Speaking from love

Follow the way of love and eagerly desire gifts of the Spirit, especially prophecy.[165]

If I have the gift of prophecy … but do not have love, I am nothing.[166]

At the heart of prophecy is the question of our heart. In my pursuit of being prophetic, there have been times God has shown me that I have prophesied from a wrong heart attitude; that is, times I have brought words to impress, self-elevate, and for my own affirmation from God and others.

One way that has helped my process has been to actively pursue love and care for people. This begins with a continual revelation of God's love for us first and from which we can speak to others from an overflow ("For the mouth speaks what the heart is full of." – Matthew 12:34). Speaking from love disempowers our

---

[165] 1 Corinthians 14:1
[166] 1 Corinthians 13:2

insecurities and places us on a secure foundation of His love and affirmation; that's a great place to prophesy from.

It is possible to be operating in the gift of prophecy with some success in terms of accuracy and fruitfulness, but when it is not grounded in love, it often doesn't last. It is an unsustainable method, because frustration and burnout inevitably come along. Sadly, I have seen this happen. Developing a sustainable method for the prophetic requires learning to love on a heart level. This can be done by actively receiving God's love and then speaking from that love.

Knowing the timing

The point at which we receive a prophetic word is not necessarily the time to give it. Learning when to give the word is where it can get interesting and comes with practice. Releasing a word in good timing is beautiful, but do not be under any pressure to get it right because God will still use it:

> So is my word that goes out from my mouth: it will not return to me empty, but will accomplish what I desire and achieve the purpose for which I sent it.[167]

There are occasions when it is appropriate to give the word after receiving it. Largely, this is when we may not get another chance to speak with someone, so we seize the opportunity. Also, I have found that it is in those moments where you receive it and with it comes a rise of faith to also release it there and then. For example, once at a Sunday service gathering, I heard God say, "In one year, this church community will have changed so much it will be unrecognisable." Given how

---

[167] Isaiah 55:11

directional it was, I thought it was best to go away and prayerfully consider it. However, a rise of faith came in the moment that stirred me to release the word right into that atmosphere and setting, so I stepped up to the front and gave the prophetic word. I kept a record of it so it could be tracked, and by the same time the next year, the leadership had changed. Also, the Sunday service location had changed, and their missional focus had significantly changed too.

On other occasions, it is right to sit on the word and hold off releasing it. It is useful then to shelve those words until you discern the right time to release them. This could be by having a paper or digital journal. I use a combination, including recording audio messages on my phone that I can refer back to, and even forward the recording when the time feels right. For example, the prophetic word for the person to leave full-time ministry and go back into teaching (in chapter three) was recorded as an audio message and had several months between receiving and releasing it.

One way our timing can be developed is by asking questions. Keep asking God when to give the word and be led by His Spirit. After giving someone the word, ask them how it sits with them, or even after a while go back and ask them if anything has changed for the word to now be relevant. Asking questions also shows that you care for them beyond the word itself.

Keep it simple

Don't overcomplicate the words you are bringing. Keep the message clear and concise. You want to communicate with the receiver in a way that they can grasp the heart of the word and not get lost in the details. There can be a place and time for labouring on the details, but generally, the aim is to deliver a message from God that they can receive well.

I've learnt the hard way not to share every part of the dream or picture I may have had, or every colour, movement and sound to the point that the recipient switches off or glazes over. Instead, I catch the core of what God is saying and then weigh what detail might be necessary to share that helps bring the word into the land for the person. Don't overcook it; keep it simple and graspable.

Just a point on simple language and, more specifically, speaking in tongues. Paul explains to the Corinth church that speaking in tongues is a wonderful spiritual gift, *but if we don't know what you're saying, why are you doing it in public?*[168] In other words, speaking in tongues is for personal edification, whereas prophesying is for public edification. The exception for speaking in tongues in public is that you pray to God to give an interpretation to share what God is saying in a language you understand. Otherwise, as Paul says, "You are just speaking into the air!"[169]

Know your measure

There are different measures when it comes to the prophetic. We have already referred to the office of the prophet[170] as being different from the gift. That is, the office carries more authority, weight and scope, and therefore operates at a different measure. Measures grow and change over time and across different

---

[168] 1 Corinthians 14:6-12
[169] 1 Corinthians 14:9
[170] Ephesians 4:11

seasons and callings in life. Knowing and understanding those measures is best found through your trusted community. There is also a balance to be found between pushing yourself to grow that measure and being careful not to overreach. Again, this is best done with healthy accountability.

The first time I heard God speak to me about someone getting pregnant certainly felt like it was beyond my measure. I had dreamt that a young couple in church leadership had a baby. I knew they had been struggling to conceive for a while, so I was trying to discern whether it was God or a pastoral desire to see them pregnant. Knowing this was potentially going to stretch my gifting and the sensitivity of it, I first went to my leader before giving the word to the couple. After weighing it together, he then encouraged me to share it. It was very much worth stretching my measure in this experience because it enabled me to reach a new level. It has been beautiful to see this word come to pass and still see their wonderful daughter today.

We do have to be very sensitive about this. For me, this was a stretching opportunity in my growth, but we must keep a pastoral check as we operate in the gift of prophecy. Generally, unless done very carefully (using the processes already mentioned), I would advise against prophesying specifics like marriages, dates of events and births – anything that might cause upset, especially if we were to get it wrong.

Interpretation

Just because we have given the prophetic word doesn't mean we know what it means or what the application is in its entirety. When releasing a word, we need to learn the discipline of not attaching our thoughts and passing them off as part of the prophecy. When giving someone a word, I often suggest what I sense the interpretation and application could be but make it clear that it is for them to weigh up and pray into it. Another option is taking someone with us so that we can 'prophesy in part'. This enables the opportunity for someone else to have the interpretation alongside the word and vice versa.

When interpreting dreams and visions, much could be discussed around symbolic numbers, colours, feelings, objects and so on. At the risk of over-simplifying the subject, I want to briefly encourage us on the importance of interpreting our dreams and visions through the lenses of the Bible, prayer and in our safe, trusted community. If you find that peace and confirmation don't come through these checks, then you can discard it as not from God. Practically speaking, as you raise your expectation to hear God this way, you could keep a journal by your bed so you can jot down and track any godly dreams.

Be creative

It is so wonderful to see the multi-faceted and multi-sensory ways we can communicate God's word to the world around us. I love this because it means, firstly, God makes prophecy accessible to us all. Secondly, prophecy comes out of our individual personalities and the unique creative ways we each have. [171] The key is not to limit ourselves to just words, though words are incredible. For instance, my friend has a powerful ministry of prophetic dancing, which is unique to her gift mix and blesses me deeply. It really wouldn't be a blessing if I danced prophetically (or otherwise)!

---

[171] Ephesians 2:10

When God speaks, take the time to look through the filter of your skill set, personality and gift mix to assess how it could be best communicated. Are you a musician, singer, actor, writer or artist? Use what you have to tell us the message that God has shown you. We really don't see this enough, and I am convinced that there is an army of creative prophetic people out there.

REFLECTION

How can you be more creative in your prophesying? Challenge yourself to begin communicating God's word creatively.

I firmly believe God wants His people to display these wonderful, creative forms of communication, so please, be bold and creative.

I hope this chapter has encouraged you to take a hands-on approach, just like taking the tool out of the toolbox, as we each pick up the gift of prophecy. Of course, it takes practice and there are processes. However, it is such a wonderful way to be used by God. So, don't delay; start today!

Did you know, the prophetic gift is not intended to remain within the context of church life? Rather, it is also meant to be displayed out there in our world. Our next chapter will explore how we can be prophetic in our world. Meanwhile, I'm feeling stirred to give fishing another go.

As you put prophecy into practice, I would love to hear your stories and testimonies, so please, do get in touch:

voice@danielcole.uk

Reflection and Activation

BIBLE REFERENCE SUMMARY

1 Corinthians 14:1, 3, 9, 29; 1 Corinthians 13:2; 2 Corinthians 4:13; Acts 12:32; Proverbs 20:5; Ezekiel 37:10; Isaiah 55:11; Ephesians 4:11, 16; Zechariah 1:13; Matthew 12:34.

SMALL GROUP DISCUSSION

1. Using the gift of prophecy is a process – what can be some of the hindrances to this process? Why is it important to understand that prophecy in and of itself isn't the end goal?

2. Give some examples of Old and New Testament prophecies and compare any differences. Read together 1 Corinthians 14:3 and take it in turn to explain which 'purpose of prophecy' you would lean towards in practice (strengthen, encourage or comfort). Share any experiences.

3. Using Proverbs 20:5, discuss how the fishing analogy (page 120) can be like prophesying. Unpack together the implications and importance of practising the prophetic.

4. "If you want to develop in the gift of prophecy, start by developing your faith." Why is faith fundamental to the gift? What could you do to increase your measure of faith in the context of the prophetic?

5. Thinking about the various creative forms of communicating God's word (music, song, acting, poetry, writing, art, etc.), what stands out to you as something you would like to develop?

MINISTRY AND ACTIVATION

1. *'How's your accuracy?' game.* You will need a bowl and something to throw in, e.g. scrunched-up paper, small balls or coins. Take turns to see who can get the item in the bowl. Maybe make it harder with smaller bowls (or cups) or stand further back. The point is, like the fishing analogy, it takes practice to improve your accuracy. It's the same with prophecy.

2. *Prayer and interpretation.* In small groups, pray for an increase of faith, after which give some time to hear God. Then share anything you heard and be ready to interpret each other's word (remember, you may have the word *or* the interpretation). Observe and talk openly about whether it is God speaking or your thoughts. Remember, this safe environment is perfect for practising. This can also be done on your own and shared with others when convenient.

3. *Creative word.* Give out some pens, pencils, felt tips, etc., and blank sheets of paper. Give some time to wait on God and draw/write poetry or song lyrics of what you felt He said. Share and explain your creative work. This can also be done on your own and shared with others when convenient.

7

Our World

Have you heard of hydrogen fuel? I have a fundamental understanding of hydrogen as an element, and as I didn't pay much attention in science class at school, my knowledge is somewhat limited! One day, God said to me, "There is going to be a breakthrough in hydrogen fuel for the domestic market so that it can be used as an alternative energy source." Given that my knowledge was lacking, this word did not mean much to me. I did some reading though, and gained helpful insight on hydrogen as a potential source of domestic fuel – if only my science teacher could see me now! I shared this word in a couple of different settings, and sometime after, I was approached by two Christian leaders in the field of business and science. They explained that in response to this word, they had teamed together to set up a company that would begin research and development. At the time of writing, they are working with a major university on a national level to break through into this whole area of using hydrogen fuel in our homes.

One of the reasons I was confident it was God's voice talking to me about hydrogen was because of the following principle: God is deeply interested in our world. He did create it after all:

The earth is the Lord's, and everything in it, the world, and all who live in it; for he founded it on the seas and established it on the waters.[172]

God's love for His world is seen at the beginning of the Bible as He designs and creates the world we now live in and the entire universe that surrounds it. We see God placed Adam and Eve in the beautiful Garden of Eden to live in its abundance. He created a sphere of influence for them to enjoy and look after.

God blessed them and said to them, "Be fruitful and increase in number; fill the earth and subdue it. Rule over the fish in the sea and the birds in the sky and over every living creature that moves on the ground."[173]

In the same way, God carefully and lovingly places us in our world today. Like the Garden of Eden, you have a sphere of influence around you where you reside, and you're encouraged to enjoy and steward it.

Circles of influence

Likening the whole world to a gigantic circle, God is deeply interested in it all on a macro level across "every tribe and language and people and nation"[174]. That's a big circle. He is also deeply interested on a micro level in every name and person – if you like, each individual circle!

That's God's worldview; how about ours? Well, imagine you have drawn a great big circle on a piece of paper and that this represents your world. Within that circle, you then draw

---

[172] Psalm 24:1-2
[173] Genesis 1:28
[174] Revelation 5:9

smaller circles representing a point of contact in your world. A circle could be members of your immediate family, next-door neighbours and work colleagues. They could be your wider family members, the checkout assistant at the local shop, the postman or the mechanic. Are you in education or part of a local community group (beyond church)? If so, there are circles within those areas as well.

Considering all the people, interests and passions that fill your life and make up those smaller circles, your world should start to look pretty full. Of course, the analogy breaks down a bit as we bring in our more distant points of contact through the internet. Social media, for example, takes this to another global level! So now, take a good look at this world of yours, filled with all those circles of influence.

Let me say this: you have a personal calling and mandate to be a voice in each of those circles, to speak into the lives of every person in those circles something about God's love that would bring transformation to them.

God's unconditional love was visible when He created the world,[175] and His love still flows today into every one of those circles you have listed. His love for your world is absolutely foundational in all we do as we reach out in our circles, especially in using our voices. With passionate, unyielding love, His voice will speak to you so you might use your voice to speak into your circles.

---

[175] John 3:16

Beyond church

Much of this book has been written with an emphasis towards a church context, which is good and proper. Sticking with the illustration, our church community should rightly make up a circle. However, we must focus on using our God-given voices to speak words that strengthen, encourage and comfort[176] in *all* our circles of influence. How limiting of us if we only function in the amazing gift of prophecy within the church when we also have a "calling and anointing given by God for ministry in all our spheres of influence"[177]! God has not called us to be a holy huddle but rather to springboard from our church circle and into our world. Do not limit our ever-speaking God, but rather listen for His voice in all areas of our lives.

REFLECTION

What thoughts come to mind when you think about using prophecy outside of church? If you haven't already, why not make a list of your circles of influence that you can begin praying over and hearing God for?

Let us then look at some biblical examples to help underline what it looks like to be prophetic in the world around us. Once we have formed a biblical framework, we will then look at how we can practically be prophetic in our spheres.

Joseph: a prophet in his world

The story of Joseph in Genesis chapters 37-50 provides some insight into how we can use our voice in the world out there.

---

[176] 1 Corinthians 14:3
[177] Bryn Jones; *Radical Church;* Destiny Image (1999)

To begin with, I would recommend pausing here and reading these passages in Genesis first.

Here is a whistle-stop tour. As a young boy, Joseph had two prophetic dreams in which he saw his family bowing down to him. They did not take it too well when he shared this word with them. In fact, they responded pretty harshly. They even planned to kill him, but he ended up being sold into slavery. He was taken from his homeland into Egypt as a slave. As a foreigner in Egypt, he then had different experiences as he tried to operate in his God-given gift for prophetic dreams. He lived in the house of Potiphar as a servant and was unjustly sent to prison. Eventually, he took up a significant national leadership role to oversee a world crisis. From slave to national leadership – only God could do this! The crux of the story is that the fulfilment of the word he received many years earlier came to fruition. His brothers came begging for food and literally bowed down before him.

There are many principles we can learn in this remarkable journey of Joseph navigating the prophetic in his home, the prison and the palace. But regarding him using his voice, I notice two themes: blessing and favour. As he encounters God's blessing and favour, he becomes a voice of blessing and favour to the world around him.

A voice of blessing

God richly and bountifully blessed Joseph as he moved about in his circles. From God's blessing flowing into Joseph, it spilt out into His world.

From the time he put him in charge of his household and of all that he owned, the LORD blessed the household of the Egyptian because of Joseph. The blessing of the LORD was on everything Potiphar had, both in the house and in the field.[178]

Everything Joseph oversaw and spoke into was blessed. He was a blessing and he spoke blessing.

Joseph's father Jacob also spoke blessing outside of his home context and in the world, as it were. There is a special moment towards the end of the story, where Jacob travels to be with his son in Egypt: "Then Joseph brought his father Jacob in and presented him before Pharaoh. After Jacob blessed Pharaoh…"[179] What a beautiful picture of the Church speaking blessing to the world: Jacob blessed Pharaoh.

Jacob blessed Pharaoh in Egypt, and God blessed Adam and Eve in the garden. On both occasions, it is the same Hebrew word used for blessing, *barak*. This is a rich Hebrew word with lots of wonderful meanings. The NAS Exhaustive Concordance defines it as "pronounce blessing", "speak", "utter" or "articulate blessing".[180] So, Jacob and Joseph, father and son, speak blessings over and into Egypt, into this circle of influence they find themselves in.

We can also bless those in our circles; that is, to 'pronounce and articulate blessings' to those we come across as we go about our daily routines. What does it look like to use your voice to be a

---

[178] Genesis 39:5
[179] Genesis 47:7
[180] 'Barak'; *NAS Exhaustive Concordance* and also *Strong's Concordance,* 1288; biblehub.com/hebrew/1288

blessing in your circles? Get practical. Raise your awareness and attentiveness to use your voice to bless and encourage others. Speaking blessing is a good filter to take stock at the end of the day and think about whether you said anything that was not a blessing to someone and then make changes accordingly.

A voice of favour

Just like God's blessing flowed from and through Joseph, God's favour was the same. Joseph experienced much favour, particularly in being prophetic in the world. Look at these three circles, for example:

- *Potiphar:* "Joseph found favour in his eyes and became his attendant."[181]
- *Prison warden:* "...the LORD ... showed him kindness and granted him favour in the eyes of the prison warden."[182]
- *Pharaoh:* "...Joseph said ... 'If I have found favour in your eyes, speak to Pharaoh for me.'"[183]

In all three circles, it is clear that he won favour in the sight of God and man.[184] Notice: *favour with man.* Having divine favour is available to us all as we seek to live as Christians in the world. Part of this is having favour with the people around us. I would like to point out that though favour comes from God, its increase is determined by how we choose to navigate

---

[181] Genesis 39:4
[182] Genesis 39:21
[183] Genesis 50:4
[184] Proverbs 3:4

our circles with other people. That's where it gets interesting, and Joseph models this well.

Joseph found favour in bringing a prophetic perspective. He was bold enough to use his prophetic gift of having and interpreting dreams in the contexts of both the prison and the palace. Bringing this unique viewpoint caused him to stand out from the crowd and get people's attention, which opened up doors of opportunity for the Kingdom to advance. Joseph did not limit or undermine his voice; instead, he brought a prophetic perspective to each circle.

We can each know God's favour as we hear His perspective in our circles, and we can know people's favour as we bring those heavenly perspectives to them.

Joseph found favour by understanding the times he was in. He was able to learn and comprehend his season and rise to the occasion. This doesn't come overnight; you cannot get a good university grade by just turning up on the first day of school. You must apply yourself by studying the subject. Joseph did this when managing Potiphar's household; he did it while serving in prison and replicated it when taking on his national role in the palace.

Consider for a moment one of your circles; for example, local or even national politics, science or technology, or your immediate neighbourhood. On a scale of one to ten, how strong is your understanding of that circle? As you begin to research, study and gain knowledge, invite God to speak into those areas and give us the solutions that would "correct the problems of our times"[185]. A small example is that whenever we've moved into a new community, Rosy will early on make a list of all our neighbours' names (even pet names!) so we can pray over them and hear God as we engage and build connections.

We can each know God's favour as we grow in understanding our circles, and we can know people's favour as we speak with understanding.

Joseph also found favour by serving. He brought solutions, wise counsel and was a faithful steward. He served those who were in charge and under his care. To serve in our circles means we must be present and available! Jesus encourages us in John 17 not to be of this world but to be in it. In fact, He commissions us into it: "As you sent me into the world, I have sent them into the world."[186] Jesus Himself came into the world "not to be served but to serve"[187]. We cannot be a voice in our circles if we are not in them; you have to be in it to win it! Ed Silvoso says, "In order to have favour with people, we need to do favours for people."[188] I would add to this by saying we also need to speak with favour too.

We can each know God's favour as we serve in our circles and people's favour as we speak with a servant's heart.

---

[185] James B. Jordon; *Christ, Opportunity and The Christian Future;* Athanasius Press (2008)

[186] John 17:18

[187] Matthew 20:28

[188] Ed Silvoso; *Transformation;* Chosen Books (2007)

Your voice of blessing and favour

I have been extremely blessed that one of my circles was in the secular workplace for twenty years before I left for a church role. Working in the property industry gave me lots of opportunities to experience God's blessing and favour and be able to use my voice to speak blessing and favour. It was one of my most fruitful circles; I actually miss the opportunities to speak blessings and favour in that sphere. How about you? Where are you speaking blessing and favour? Let's all use our voices to brim over with blessing and know God's incredible, incomparable favour as we speak into each of our circles.

REFLECTION

Consider putting some time aside to study and gain knowledge about a particular circle that might position you to speak into it. Or consider whether there is a circle you could devote some energy and resources to serving that would prepare you to speak in.

Jesus: a prophet in His world

Let's continue building a biblical framework for what it looks like to be prophetic in the world. Jesus, like Joseph, was a prophet. Jesus was sent into the world to bring the Father's voice to us.

> For God so loved the world that he gave his one and only Son, that whoever believes in him shall not perish but have eternal life. For God did not send his Son into

the world to condemn the world, but to save the world through him.[189]

In being sent, Jesus displayed for us how to speak into this world. Jesus was an expert at seamlessly moving between different circles of people and speaking into the lives of those around Him. He would have a firm word for the religious leaders[190], a wise word for the financial sector[191] and a gracious word for the sinner[192]. Whatever sphere He entered, He would carry a prophetic mandate to speak life and reveal the Father's love. Jesus also gave some good pieces of advice to help us speak into our world. Let me share two.

YOU ARE THE SALT OF THE EARTH

Rosy can sometimes take offence when I sprinkle salt on the meal she has cooked! She is determined that the meal is just right, whereas my attempt to justify the salt is that I am simply enhancing the flavour she has skilfully already brought together! In my defence, this is the precise role of salt: to brighten up the flavours.

Jesus advises that, like salt, we should be those that enhance and brighten up the world around us. This can be done through our actions and our words. Words that carry love and speak life into our circles will bring enhancing transformation to the lives of those around us and ultimately bring them into a new or deeper relationship with Jesus.

---

[189] John 3:16-17
[190] Matthew 3:7
[191] Luke 19:1-27
[192] John 8:10-11

THE KINGDOM OF HEAVEN IS LIKE YEAST

Yeast is the active agent that causes dough to rise and develop into a spongy texture. In the same way, we are Kingdom agents sent into our world to 'work through the dough'. Like yeast, our words can cause people to rise and develop into their God-given purposes. Yeast is not an idle agent but is proactively at work, bringing the other ingredients together to form the dough. Likewise, being prophetic in our circles requires actively being alert to hear God's word and then actively using ours.

Salt and yeast in your world

Speaking with 'salt' and 'yeast' makes what we say simple and accessible to us all. I like simplicity. A simple word of encouragement in the office, a word of kindness at the school gate or a word of comfort to a neighbour are all opportunities to bring God's love and life into our circles. Being salt and yeast is about speaking words that carry a heavenly perspective into our neighbourhoods. It's speaking godly wisdom and supernatural strategies into our marketplace spheres, such as business, education and healthcare.

When my friend, a Christian businessman, was setting up his factory for his expanding business, the advice was to set up a factory in China because of the financial benefits. However, he believed he had heard God say to set it up in Manchester, UK instead. Although this did not make business sense to others, he trusted God's strategy. Within a few years, his sales went global and way beyond their expectations. The customer feedback from the staggering sales was that the products carried extra credibility because they were 'Made in England'. Because of his success, he has been able to create local jobs and invest in the local economy.

As you go about your circles, be open to God to speak to you about individuals you relationally connect with, and ask Him about the circles as a whole. Use your voice to speak about business strategies, financial solutions, creative communications, medical breakthroughs, environmental impacts and community initiatives. Prayerfully look at your circles and ask, "How can I be salt and yeast as I hear God and use my voice?"

You: prophetic in your world

Now we have a biblical basis from Joseph and Jesus, let's get practical about using your voice in your world.

Most of the practicalities already covered in chapter six can apply to our various settings outside the church. The overall key is to adapt our communication and make it appropriate for the setting. For example, it would be pretty weird if I suddenly interrupted a friendly conversation with a colleague, cleared my throat, put on a holy voice and said, "Thus says the Lord..."!

What's interesting in both of Jesus's analogies of salt and yeast[193] is how covert they are. His encouragement is not to brashly or overtly exert ourselves into our relationships and bring the prophetic gift through loud and booming voices. Instead, there is something relational and warm about faithfully impacting our circles by hearing God and using our voices in these spheres.

---

[193] Matthew 5:13; Matthew 13:33

One of the earlier times of using my voice in the world was when an older lady got my attention in the queue at the bank. Feeling a stirring to bring her encouragement, I finished up at the bank and rushed out to then see her walking down the high street. I caught up with her, tapped her on the shoulder and nervously said, "Hi, I'm from a local church and felt God say that He loves you." Then came the awkward split-second pause, which felt like a lifetime, as I awaited her response. My vision and faith, at the moment, was that she would say, "What must I do to be saved?" and have some kind of powerful encounter. Then those walking past us on the high street would overhear and also repent, with hundreds coming to know Jesus, all on my lunch break! Instead, she replied with, "That's good of him!" and walked off into a shop. I hastily walked off in embarrassment, hoping nobody had noticed!

Bringing words to strangers might work for others, but when I consider the prophetic words I've brought in my various circles (outside of a church context), I would say 80% of them have been within some level of relationship. There would be a basis of connection as I got to know someone, from which I would catch God's heart for them. Out of that relationship, I then felt able to speak into their life from a place of love and desire to see them fulfilled.

As we have covered, prophecy in a church context works best in relational connection. It's the same anywhere else. Of course, if using your voice is not particularly in a relational setting but is still motivated by love and has good results, that's fantastic. Keep operating in line with your personality and character, and be true to who you are. Kris Vallotton rightly says that "it takes all kinds of prophets to transform the world"[194]; so it is important to honour each other in our differing approaches as we speak into our circles and bring godly transformation.

Okay then, here are three practical pointers to help you be prophetic in your world.

1. KEEP THE CONVERSATION GOING

Our aim shouldn't be to bring 'mic drop / mind blown' intense, one-off words; rather, through ongoing conversation, we should be able to keep our channels open and our voice ready. Removing that sense of intensity will take the pressure off the one giving the word and also any pressure from the recipient having to respond in the moment.

Keeping the conversation flowing allows you to also be part of the process with them, which could lead them to Jesus. Ask questions, ask for feedback, and be real and authentic. There is trust and love in a healthy relationship which flows both ways and creates the perfect setting for God to speak through you. Using this covert conversational style of prophesying in the world reveals your love for the person over and above everything else. If you have started a conversation with someone new – perhaps you get chatting with someone on the bus/train/plane and are able to speak a word of encouragement to them – then you could offer to swap contact details to keep the connection going (if you feel safe to do so).

---

[194] Kris Vallotton; *School of Prophets;* Chosen Books (2015)

2. CHOOSE YOUR LANGUAGE

As we are having those God-inspired conversations, we must drop the 'Christianese'. Learn to take out our familiar Christian phrases and words to talk in a way that is relevant to the listener. It's being naturally supernatural as we weave God's thoughts into those conversations. In my role as a Property Manager, I had a team of contractors who worked for me, one of whom was a young plumber. After getting to know this plumber more, and sensing God's voice for him, one day I said something along the lines of, "When you were speaking about your career prospects and how you didn't see much progression, I want you to know that you are more than a plumber and I can see you as a leader. I strongly think you should consider doing some training in site management." I spoke what I was prophetically burdened with regarding his future in a simple way that he could hear and relate to.

3. DISCERN THE RESPONSE

Discernment means being able to distinguish or recognise what might be hard to see. With the guidance of the Holy Spirit, we can discern how one might respond to the word. After giving the word, you may discern a hard, closed response, so you may choose to just release this to them and God. On the other hand, you may discern a soft, open response and choose to build on it and explore it with them.

My plumber colleague was initially resistant and even scoffed at me a little, so I felt it right to leave the conversation alone and let him ponder over it. A few weeks later, he brought it up with me, and we were then able to talk it through as he questioned further. It gave me a chance to introduce the faith element and explain it was God that spoke.

Go into your world

From a passionate love for the world, God sent Jesus, who set a precedent for us by sending His Spirit into our world. Therefore, prophecy is not only for those within the church community but should be exercised in every circle in which we find ourselves every day.

As we move about in our circles with everyday adventures and learning to hear His voice and use ours, I am filled with excitement. I imagine a multitude of people, young and old, men and women – a beautiful symphony of voices – all communicating God's love and power. These voices are deployed and impacting society at all levels, bringing transformational love and power. So, let each of us, as Kingdom agents, bring in the rule and reign of our Lord Jesus by taking up the prophetic gift into our world.

Reflection and Activation

BIBLE REFERENCE SUMMARY

Genesis 1:28; Genesis 37-50; Proverbs 3:4; Matthew 5:13; Matthew 13:33; John 17:18.

SMALL GROUP DISCUSSION

1. It can be daunting to bring someone a word outside the church context. Can you share any experiences or examples of how you found it easy or nerve-racking?

2. Read Proverbs 3:4. What does it look like to find favour with man? How could you grow and develop your favour in your spheres of influence?

3. What are the implications for your voice when you consider that Jesus has sent you into our world? (John 17:18.)

4. When it comes to being prophetic in the world, covert is better than overt. Do you agree? (Matthew 5:13; 13:13.)

MINISTRY AND ACTIVATION

1. *Who is in your circles?* Draw a large circle on a piece of paper. This circle represents your world. Start to fill this circle with lots of other smaller circles that would each represent parts of your life where you would connect with people. If there is space, try to also put people's names in the smaller circles so that it is personal. Discuss your drawings with others and how you could be a voice of influence in those circles. Pin this paper up to be reminded to prayerfully ask God for words in those circles.

2. *Practice.* Giving a word to someone who is not yet a Christian can be challenging as we often rely on 'Christianese'. Try some role-playing whereby you each take turns to share your testimony without using overtly religious terms. This can be a fun activity that can help us use language that relates to the listener.

3. *Prayer.* Use John 17:18 as a basis and pray that we would be filled with the power of the Holy Spirit to be sent afresh into our circles, ready to display God's love by speaking words of life. Pray that we would know a new discernment for those around us and that each would take up the prophetic gift and bring in the rule and reign of our Lord Jesus by being His Kingdom agents to our world.

8

An Invitation

...there before me was a door standing open in heaven.
And the voice I had first heard...[195]

In chapter two, we looked at 'why' God speaks, and we started
with the first book of the Bible, Genesis. As we wrap things up,
I want to give some final thoughts from the last book of the
Bible, Revelation. It's actually more like one thought, really,
and that is an invitation – an invitation to take up this
wonderful gift of prophecy.

Claudia Severa

Sending out invitations, even in my short lifetime, has changed
drastically. I remember in my younger years when invites would
simply come in the post. Then things progressed to email
invites, after which social media invites became a thing. And
just last night, we received a birthday party invite via instant
messaging! What will be next?

Well, before smartphones, emails and even the postal service,
there were wooden tablets and carbon ink. In fact, among the
oldest handwritten documents in Britain is a birthday party

---

[195] Revelation 4:1

invitation. It dates back to around the first century and was found by excavators in 1973 at a Roman settlement in Northumberland, England. The invite is from one sister to another:

> Claudia Severa to her Lepidina, greetings. On 11 September, sister, for the day of the celebration of my birthday, I give you a warm invitation to make sure that you come to us, to make the day more enjoyable for me by your arrival, if you are present.[196]

Perhaps we should go back to wooden tablets?

Before Claudia's birthday party and wooden tablets, invitations were given by voice, particularly those in high society, such as royal families and the very wealthy. They used a large network of servants to transmit their invites via oral proclamation.[197] A tedious yet important job. For example, getting the intimate and intricate invitation details wrong could cause a whole host of problems, such as resulting in attending formal high society weddings in a fancy dress costume, or travelling for many miles on horse and carriage to find it was the wrong date and time!

Voice invitations actually go as far back as Scripture, where there is a clear invitational theme from God to us. God uses His voice and the voices of His heaven-sent messengers to give us invitations. God uses His voice when He presents to John His invitation.

---

[196] archaeology.org.issues/106-1309/artifact/1171-writing-tablet-roman-fort-northumberland
[197] odacreative.com/blog/2018/12/24/celebrating-famous-invitations-from-acient-to-modern-times

Revelation

A quick backdrop. John, the writer of Revelation, starts the book by describing how he is confined to the island of Patmos because he preaches the gospel.[198] Next, he writes of his suffering and imprisonment. He then describes how he hears God's voice like a trumpet and his visitation of Christ within this context.[199] Going into the second and third chapters, we read of John receiving prophetic messages for seven churches. We then come to Revelation 4:1, which is where I want us to pause.

> After this I looked, and there before me was a door standing open in heaven. And the voice I had first heard speaking to me like a trumpet said, "Come up here, and I will show you what must take place after this."

John goes from a heavenly visitation to receiving a heavenly invitation.

Come up here

God's invitation to John is to "come". It's an invitation for you too: to come deeper into your relationship of hearing His voice and using yours.

Back to party invitations. Like Claudia to her sister, when somebody invites you to "come to my party", there are certain feelings attached when receiving it. Extroverts are perhaps excited, jubilant and eager for the day to arrive. Introverts may have feelings of trepidation and anxiety and look for excuses to

---

[198] Revelation 1:9
[199] Revelation 1:10

decline. Regarding the birthday invite we received last night via instant messaging, I am planning to be poorly that day.

With God, the invite to "come" is said with such simplicity. Come just as you are. Come with confidence, not in your ability or efforts, but in His. Bring the real, authentic 'you' and come. "Come up here," where He wants to show you things of His nature and your destiny; up here to higher levels of revelation and heavenly perspectives; up here to greater depths of His heart and desires for the Church and our world. Hear His invitation to you today to "come up here".

This is an invitation to the prophetic as well: "…I will show you what must take place after this…" God wants to show you things that haven't happened yet – a heavenly, prophetic perspective – showing you glimpses of your future and of those around you.

My question is, will you accept His invitation to the prophetic?

The gift of prophecy was birthed in the heart of God and distributed to us by His Spirit. Therefore, it is His plan (not ours) to give each of us, like John, an invitation to "come" and step more into the prophetic.

Let's further examine Revelation 4:1, from which I want to pull out three characteristics of God's prophetic invitation, as we consider our response and possible next steps.

1. AN OPEN INVITATION

   …a door standing open in heaven…

In March 2018, the much anticipated and prestigious wedding invitations of Prince Harry and Meghan Markle were sent out to 600 people. These were no ordinary invites and were made with intricate detail and design. Using American ink on English paper, the invite producer used a 1930s printing press to firstly die-stamp in gold and then, secondly, to bevel and gild the edges. These were not mass-produced, but each one was created individually.[200] Sadly, I, along with millions of other hopefuls, did not receive one of these invites. The media reported that the Thames Valley police force conducted their biggest ever operation for this wedding, largely for this single purpose: to stop those not invited from getting in.

John shows us that with God, the door is very much standing open. You are invited and you can get in. This vision of a door standing open is one of my favourite pictures in the Bible. It is a wonderful metaphor for His grace. A threshold that we can each step through by grace, allowing us entry into the supernatural realm, which is where the prophetic operates from. If we ever feel a distance between God and us, I can tell you, the door stands open, and there is a free invitation to enter by His grace.

Have you ever felt times when you have struggled to hear His voice and maybe begun to doubt that God would speak to you or even want to use your voice? Please, know the door is standing open and His voice of grace invites you afresh. Sometimes, I think we can struggle with this open door of grace, and we must remind ourselves that through the death and resurrection of Jesus, His warm and embracing invitation to want to speak with us is always available.

---

[200] royal.uk/invitations-wedding-prince-harry-and-ms-meghan-markle-have-been-issued

He does indeed place before us an open door that no one can shut,[201] but sometimes we can turn our back to it. Blockages can come and prevent us from experiencing that open door, such as losing the habit of staying connected to Him or sin that may have crept in. Well, there is something we can do about that: repent. Repentance literally means to turn around from one direction to another.[202] As we say sorry to God for those blockages, we turn away from them and towards the open door of grace. By His grace, an invitation has been dispatched to come and step over the threshold and freely approach His throne of grace[203] to hear His beautiful voice as He speaks from limitless love, wisdom, knowledge and revelation.

As we pursue the gift of prophecy, please don't limit hearing God's voice or using your voice to natural ability, personality type, feelings, circumstances or character. Instead, grasp His grace. Each of us is given an open invitation to be prophetic, not because of our efforts and attempts to earn it, but simply by His grace.[204]

Practical next steps:

- Invite God to show you any barriers, like wrong mindsets or heart attitudes that would prevent you from stepping through the open door of grace and into further prophetic ministry.
- With the gift of prophecy in mind, do a Bible study on grace (maybe through the Epistles).

---

[201] Revelation 3:8
[202] Acts 3:19
[203] Hebrews 4:16
[204] Romans 12:6

- After you have brought someone a prophetic word, get into the practice of taking a moment to give thanks to God for choosing to partner with you by His grace.

2. AN INVITATION FOR MORE

…the voice I had first heard…

I like that John here describes the similarity to when Jesus 'first' spoke to him in Revelation 1:9 (like a trumpet). He is making it abundantly clear that hearing the voice of God wasn't a one-off occurrence but was repeated. It doesn't stop there, as the Book of Revelation describes John hearing God in a plethora of ways as He communicates many messages to him about the future of the Church, His Kingdom and our world. This reveals to us God's desire to be in ongoing communication with us. There is so much more for us to hear!

Similar to John, you too may be able to recollect the 'first' time you heard God, but I can tell you it won't be the last. Please, don't limit the voice of God in either what He is saying or how He is saying it. He will speak to you in familiar ways and surprise you with new ways too. This 'invitation for more' isn't just to hear His voice increasingly, but also in terms of developing our voice as well. Let this 'invitation for more' springboard you into action. Find ways to pursue and increase His voice and yours. How can you step into your next level and new measure as you pursue the worthy pursuit of prophecy?

Practical next steps:

- Seek resources to inspire and 'fan into flames' the gift within you. Then, regularly give time to receive these resources.

- Increase your prayer time so you can (a) ask God to speak more and (b) listen more to His voice.
- Use some of the practical tips in this book to develop and grow using your voice. Try some new and creative ways of using your voice. Don't limit yourself, and seek feedback.

3. A SHARED INVITATION

    ...speaking to me like a trumpet...

This voice that John hears is described as the sound of a trumpet. We will circle back to the significance of the trumpet shortly. For now, I want to draw out one of the purposes of a trumpet, which is to gather people. Scripture shows it being used for gathering people together for battle[205], corporate worship[206] and communicating important messages[207].

In this same way, we too can hear the trumpet sound of His voice calling us to gather and share in His invitation. It is not an isolated invite but a joint experience where we can assemble with others as we hear His voice and use ours in the community.

I have already covered the importance of being in a prophetic community. However, what's interesting in this Revelation 4 passage is that one of the first things John sees as he enters the throne room of God is community: "Surrounding the throne were twenty-four other thrones, and seated on them were

---

[205] Numbers 10:9; 1 Corinthians 14:8
[206] 2 Chronicles 29:28
[207] 1 Samuel 13:3

twenty-four elders."[208] Here is a picture of God's people gathering around the throne to worship Him and hear His voice together. It is from this place of gathering around God, who is at the centre, that we can see each other through the throne. This is where we catch God's heart of blessing and encouragement towards a person through the lens of His throne and, from that revelation, speak into their lives. Yes, His voice is personal and individual, but it is meant to be explored and practised in a shared context.

Practical next steps:

- Whom can you approach to form your community? This could be a peer you can grow with in the prophetic, a mentor who brings guidance, or ideally, it could be both.
- Find opportunities to practise in a group setting where you might get feedback and learn together. This healthy culture of practice can breed development and maturity.
- Why not use this or another book and explore prophecy as a small group?

God's voice invitation to "come and step into the prophetic" remains open. There is always more to develop, and it is a shared invite to explore together. Now, let me share some geeky trumpet knowledge as I take us on a little trumpet tangent.

---

[208] Revelation 4:4

His voice: like a trumpet

Did you know the trumpet originates in heaven? The first recording of the trumpet sound was from heaven down towards the earth.

> On the morning of the third day there was thunder and lightning, with a thick cloud over the mountain, and a very loud trumpet blast. Everyone in the camp trembled.[209]

The trumpet's metallic, vibrating and alerting sound was never heard by human ears up to this point. Then Moses and the Israelites heard this unfamiliar sound blasting from the open skies, and I am sure it frightened the life out of them. If that wasn't enough, the passage in Exodus 19 says that the trumpet's sound grew louder and louder, and then Moses spoke and God answered Him.[210] What an intense sound that must have been!

John, in Revelation, hears God's loud voice like this trumpet sound. One commentator suggests that the trumpet sound of God's voice was "peculiarly proper to proclaim the coming of the great King, and his victory over all his enemies"[211]. In other words, His voice, like a trumpet sound, was synonymous with victory.

Like the Israelites hearing the unveiling of the trumpet on the third day, Jesus rose from the grave in victory also on the third day. One heavenly trumpet blasts to the next, as Jesus

---

[209] Exodus 19:16
[210] Exodus 19:19
[211] *Joseph Benson's Commentary of the Old and New Testaments; Patristic Publishing (2019)*

overcomes death and all the evil powers to become the ultimate, eternal victorious King.

If Jesus overcoming death once and for evermore is not enough, what about all the prophetic foreshadows of God's voice of victory in the Old Testament? Consider all the other trumpet blasts like the stories of Joshua, Gideon and David, as they saw mighty victories. Let these stories give you hope that we have victory in His voice.

His trumpet blasts of victory can be heard today. His voice proclaims miracles in the hardships and breakthroughs in the impossible. His voice announces hope in the valley and peace in the storm. His voice affirms that His Kingdom is truly being established and extended here on earth as it is in heaven. Let His voice of victory speak to you like a trumpet.

Our voice: like a trumpet

Another piece of trivia on the trumpet. Did you know the trumpet is the only instrument recorded in Scripture that was specifically designed and commissioned by God?

> The LORD said to Moses "Make two trumpets of hammered silver…"[212]

Though it was first designed and used in heaven, the instrument was then entrusted to us to make and then use. It was meant for our lips so we could put it into practice; a beautiful picture of our voices being intricately designed and uniquely commissioned by God. He has wonderfully and intentionally created us to have a distinctive, prophetic voice. Your voice has

---

[212] Numbers 10:1-2

been sealed with His stamp of approval, so go for it: sound the trumpet blast!

The great prophetic partnership

This final invitation is not for spectating but for participating in the gift of prophecy. We are called to partner with God Himself, step on the pitch and play our part. It's like football (all good analogies can be found in football!) – eleven players with one mission: score goals and win the game. Throughout the match, the players will use their voices to challenge and encourage each other. They will listen to the manager's voice for new instructions and guidance. They each listen and use their voices to communicate and flow in partnership as a team. For my own sanity, I won't go into when players don't use their voice and communication breakdowns can cost the match! The point is, get in the game. Partner with the manager to hear his voice and then use your voice as you navigate through the pitch, which will ultimately help accomplish the mission.

In chapter two, I have written about the first recorded words of God found in Genesis. This, then, is the final prophecy of the Bible:

> The Spirit and the bride say, "Come!" And let the one who hears say, "Come!" Let the one who is thirsty come; and let the one who wishes take the free gift of the water of life.[213]

Just as John hears God's voice telling him to come, this same invitation is for the whole Church (the Bride). More than that, though, because the invite extends further; it's not just an

---

[213] Revelation 22:17

invitation to come but also to speak the same words and say to others, "Come!" It is a partnership in which you and I, as the invited, can also be the invitation-givers. It is a great prophetic partnership with God. What a privilege to be counted in, be on the team and play our part!

At the heart of each prophetic word we bring, in partnership with God, can ultimately be an invitation for others to 'come'. That might be someone coming into a new relationship with God at salvation, as they experience the water of life for the first time. It might be calling someone to come deeper into the water of life and enter new measures of their relationship with God. The invitation applies to anyone who wishes to receive from the water of life, whether at the shallow or deep end. That's the beauty of God's open invitation and the wonder of this great prophetic partnership.

Will you join me in this exhilarating invitation of partnering with God to hear His voice and use ours? What an invitation! Would you count yourself as part of this harmonious chorus of God's voice and yours? A joining of voices so profoundly synchronised and intimately connected as we speak out in perfect unison, "Come!" In a nutshell, my friend, that is what hearing His voice and using ours is all about. This is prophecy.

Epilogue

Through this book, you will have picked up on my heart for the prophetic being in community, and hopefully, you will continue to (or begin to) put into practice some of those thoughts. Exploring the gift of prophecy together is the best way to grow in this area. In fact, the book has been laid out purposefully so that chapters two to seven can be used as a six-week course where you can get together with some friends or your church small group.

VOICE small groups

This is another opportunity to journey with others, by signing up for a VOICE small group. These will be six-week online courses at various times of the year where we will help you grow and develop in the gift of prophecy in your context. So, send an email to *voice@danielcole.uk* to express an interest and a sign-up form will be sent to you – or simply scan the QR code below.

Finally, on the page overleaf you will see the Voice Check Assessment for you to complete. This is identical to the one you did in the Introduction, so you can compare your results to celebrate growth areas and highlight areas for further development.

Voice Check Assessment

Give yourself a score between 1 (low) and 10 (high). Once you have a total, read through the score results. Complete it instinctively, giving your gut responses rather than overthinking it. The goal is to help you find areas of strength and growth.

GOD'S VOICE

Hearing God comes quite easily to me.

(1) (2) (3) (4) (5) (6) (7) (8) (9) (10)

I strongly understand why God chooses to speak to me.

(1) (2) (3) (4) (5) (6) (7) (8) (9) (10)

I can identify God speaking to me in various ways.

(1) (2) (3) (4) (5) (6) (7) (8) (9) (10)

I listen to God by intentionally putting specific time aside.

(1) (2) (3) (4) (5) (6) (7) (8) (9) (10)

I listen to God as I go about my day in conversation with Him.

(1) (2) (3) (4) (5) (6) (7) (8) (9) (10)

Add the scores together to give you a total: _____

Scores of 5-10

There are some areas needing attention to unlock more of hearing His voice.

Scores of 11-25

There is some understanding and experience in hearing God; however, more can be developed.

Scores of 26-37

You have a good understanding and some good practices in hearing God. Consider some tweaks to go to a new level.

Scores of 38-45

You are extremely attentive, intentional and creative in hearing God often. Find ways to help others.

Scores of 46-50

You imitate Jesus – always hearing the Father's voice!

YOUR VOICE

I am quite confident in using my voice.

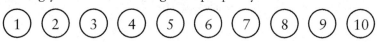

What I say and my faith are closely connected.

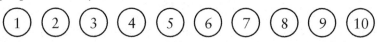

I strongly understand the 'gift of prophecy'.

(1) (2) (3) (4) (5) (6) (7) (8) (9) (10)

I have trusted people around me to help me practise the prophetic safely.

(1) (2) (3) (4) (5) (6) (7) (8) (9) (10)

I understand the power of using my voice outside of the church context.

(1) (2) (3) (4) (5) (6) (7) (8) (9) (10)

Add the scores together to give you a total: _____

Scores of 5-10

There are some areas needing attention to unlock more of using your voice.

Scores of 11-25

Though you've had some experience being prophetic, there is more to develop.

Scores of 26-37

You often use the gift of prophecy and have confidence in using your voice. Consider some tweaks to go to a new level.

Scores of 38-45

You are very confident about using your voice. Connect with others and find trusted people.

Scores of 46-50

You imitate Jesus – always speaking the Father's words!

Acknowledgements

I leaned heavily on my close circles to help shape the book's premise, content, flow and theology. It has been very much a team effort, and I would not have completed this project without gifted and generous input from such supportive people. There are many to thank but I wanted to honour a few in particular.

A big thank you to Dr David and Philippa Emmett, who have been our spiritual parents for many years, always believing in us and spurring us on, which includes encouragement and guidance with this book.

Thanks to John and Marion Kendrick and Phil Aldis for your ever-helpful insights, rich knowledge and many hours of line editing – you were very patient with me!

Thank you to my KingsGate Community Church family for welcoming us with overwhelming love and support. It's being in such an inspiring, faith-filled Kingdom culture that gave me the confidence to pursue this dream.

A big thanks to Rosy for graciously and sacrificially stepping into the gaps as I gave attention to this project. Also, for being brave enough to provide me with hard-to-hear feedback when needed (though I wasn't always thankful in the moment!)

Finally, as I look back at my life, I would be voiceless and fearful if it were not for God's grace and mercy. Thank you, Father, for your transforming love that set me free and gave me a voice that can be used for your glory.

Printed in Great Britain
by Amazon